The Country Journal Woodburner's Cookbook

The Country Journal

Illustrated by Margot Apple

Woodburner's Cookbook

How to Cook and Bake—and Save Energy—
on an Airtight Wood Stove

Janet Bachand Chadwick

Country Journal Publishing Company   1981

Also by Janet Chadwick

HOW TO LIVE ON ALMOST NOTHING AND HAVE PLENTY:
A Practical Introduction to Small-Scale Sufficient Country Living (1979)

Library of Congress Cataloguing in Publication Data

Chadwick, Janet, 1933-
  The Country journal woodburner's cookbook.

  Includes index.
  1. Cookery. 2. Stoves, Wood. I. Blair & Ketchum's country journal. II. Title.
TX652.C475   641.5'8   81-3186
                                     AACR2

ISBN 0-393-01503-3
ISBN 0-393-00076-1 (pbk.)

Manufactured in the United States of America
First Edition
3, 4, 5, 6, 7, 8, 9, 0

To my husband Raymond and our children
Karen Chadwick Marcelino, Gary, David, Mary, and Kimberley,
whose love of good food has been
a constant challenge to my creative ability.

CONTENTS

Acknowledgments ix

1 **The Method**
Why and How to Use Your Airtight Stove
    for Cooking and Baking—
    and the Equipment You'll Need

29 **The Recipes**

31 *Basics*
Sauces and Stocks 32
Toppings, Stuffings and Seasonings 40
Pastry 43

47 *Soups*

57 *Meatless Soups*

63 *Main Dishes*
Beef 64
Pork 79
Poultry and Rabbit 88
Seafood and Fish 104
Italian Specialties 115
Meatless Dishes 123

129 *Vegetables*

139 *Breads*

151 *Desserts*
Cakes 152
Frostings 162
Cookies 164
Pies 167
Puddings 171

Index 177

A cookbook requires many hours of hard work, and many helping hands are needed along the way. Unfortunately it isn't possible to thank everyone personally, but there are those who should have recognition.

I would especially like to thank my editors, Jane Garrett and Anne Eberle, not only for their expertise in the publishing field but for their encouragement and never-failing friendship. A special thanks, too, to Margot Apple, whose sketches so clearly explain my instructions.

I would like to thank Lynn Liberty of the Garden Way Living Center in Burlington, Vermont, for asking me to do the woodstove cooking demonstration at which the birth of the idea for this book took place, and Vermont Castings of Randolph, Vermont, for making a Vigilant woodstove available to me for recipe testing.

My family always plays a large part in my work, and so I'd like to thank my mother Florence Bachand and my sister Constance Mahaney for their help in going through the archives of our family recipes to find our favorites for this book. Thank you to my daughters Kim for washing mountains of pots and pans, Mary for her assistance during the typing, and Karen for her help in copying the final manuscript. I certainly can't leave out my husband Ray and our sons Gary and David for taking over my regular chores here at Sunnybrook while I wrote this book.

Janet Bachand Chadwick

Sunnybrook
Monkton, Vermont
October 1, 1980

THE METHOD

Why and How to Use Your Airtight Stove for Cooking and
Baking—and the Equipment You'll Need

No matter how you look at the energy situation, conservation is the answer. While the reasons for the energy crunch are numerous and complex, it is clear that until our demand for energy is no longer greater than the ready supply, shortages and rising costs will continue to plague us.

In many ways, each of us is in a position to take some responsibility for working toward this improved relationship of supply and demand. We can make each unit of energy that we use work in more than one way. This book will show you how, if you even partially heat your home with a wood or coal stove, you can use the same heat source for cooking a remarkable variety of foods.

"Sure," you say, "we've stir-fried some things and made good soups on our woodstove from time to time. Works fine." Of course it does, but a lot of your tastiest cooking ordinarily involves the oven, a big energy spender in most kitchens. **Now there is a way to** *bake* **on the top of wood and coal heaters or on a single surface unit of an electric or gas stove, or even on a hot plate.** As this book shows, this kind of baking can be done so reliably, with a little practice, that you can confidently produce breads, cakes, casseroles, meat roasts, quiches and other pies for company, using little or no energy beyond what is already heating your home.

The text of this book would appear to address the owners of wood or coal heaters, but all the recipes can be cooked using any heat source. **Temperature control of your pan is the key, not the source of heat.** All you need is a heater with a flat surface on which a pan can be placed.

By all means, continue to cook soups and stews on your woodburner. In fact, I'm going to give you some of my favorite recipes to add to your collection. But don't let that be the end of it! You can go on to cook delicious foods that are usually baked in the oven.

If you don't have a wood or coal heater with a suitable cooking surface, you will still save energy by using the techniques described, provided you use only 1 or 2 burners of a gas, electric, or oil stove, as compared with using a standard oven. (If you use more than 2 stovetop burners, you would do better to cook several foods at once in a regular oven.)

If you choose to, **you can in fact use your standard oven for any of the book's recipes for baking.** Simply use the baking temperature specified in the recipe and bake for the recommended length of time **plus 10 minutes** (to allow for the different ratio of food to heated space when several foods are cooked at once). Many of the recipes (such as those for soups and stews using a direct heat source, not those involving baking) can also be cooked in a Crock-Pot (see p. 25).

In warmer areas of our country where wood and coal heaters are not needed, there are still many opportunities to save energy in baking by using techniques described here. Oven cooking increases the temperature inside the house. On hot days, in order to bake in the oven, you must turn on the air conditioner or the fans to make it bearable. Baking on top of the stove reduces the need for these large energy-consuming appliances, while using fewer units for the actual baking itself.

Where It All Began

Before our present house had been built on our country property, we decided to camp there for a few days in a tent. Like all campers, we planned to cook over an open fire or a charcoal grill. My father-in-law came with us, and neither he nor my husband Ray was particularly fond of charcoal-cooked foods. They leaned heavily toward old-fashioned home cooking, and plenty of it.

I am a curious person by nature and I love a challenge, so I decided to try a full-course meal on my charcoal grill. The menu went like this: fried chicken, mashed potatoes, corn on the cob, tossed salad, homemade bread, chocolate cream pie, milk and coffee. It seemed reasonable to expect that I would be able to cook the potatoes and corn in regular pans right on top of the grill, since the grill was a good source of heat. The salad needed no cooking, the chicken could be fried in my heavy cast-iron pan on top of the grill, so that left the chocolate pudding, bread and piecrust.

I was sure I could rig up some sort of double boiler, using small stones to hold one pot above the water in another pot to give me the same type of cooking temperature I would have in a double boiler at home. My ice chest would be fine to cool the pudding. Actually the biggest challenge would be the piecrust and the homemade bread.

I gave a great deal of thought to the type of heat required for baking these items. **Oven heat is dry, therefore must be vented; it must circulate freely so that foods are cooked evenly from all sides,** and for piecrust and bread, it had to be reasonably hot. The only thing that I had with me that I felt would do was a 4-quart cast-iron Dutch oven. Because I didn't have a round cake rack with me, I had to improvise some method of keeping my baking dish off the bottom of the pan. Otherwise, heat could not circulate freely and cook evenly from all sides, and the bottom of my bread or crust would burn. I solved this by using small flat stones again. I was confident about raising the temperatures inside the pan high enough to bake. There was the additional problem caused by the structure of the inside of the cast-iron cover. The pan was made for moist cooking, and the small nodes inside the cover caused moisture to drop back down on the food inside. Something had to be done to prevent this. The solution was to line the cover of the pan with tinfoil, with the shiny side facing back down into the pan. Now the heat would come up the sides of the pan and be reflected back down on the food that was baking. Next I had to find a way to vent my little oven. Because of its small size, it didn't seem to require too much venting, so I decided to try my first venture by using a small teaspoon between the cover and the pan.

Because I ordinarily preheated my oven at home to bake piecrust, I put my little makeshift oven on the hot grill to heat up for 15 minutes before I carefully slipped my piecrust into it. I quickly covered the pan and vented it with a teaspoon. I waited for approximately the usual baking time before I peeked, and sure enough, my piecrust was baked perfectly. It had even browned slightly, and I hadn't expected that. Meanwhile I had put my bread dough into a round cake pan to rise. When it had doubled in bulk, I again slipped it quickly into the little oven, proceeded as before, and baked a very nice loaf of bread. Needless to say, that meal was the talk of our family for some time to come and is still mentioned frequently.

Stovetop Baking Arrives

Once you know that you can use your wood or coal heater in cold weather and a single burner the rest of the year, the few pieces of equipment you need to cook this way, such as a cast-iron Dutch oven, a couple of stovetop thermometers, and a few round baking dishes, become even more practical. Today I cook on my woodstove whenever it's going and do all small baked items on the top of the gas stove when the woodstove isn't in use. I've learned what ingredients help to make the recipes most successful, and I've got the method of temperature control down to a science. I've also found that it is possible to use many items I already have on hand to save money on baking dishes. These are described in another section (see p. 9).

A few friends have raised objections to cooking on wood or coal heaters that might not be located in the kitchen area. They're largely concerned about spatters, but these can be controlled with a spatter screen. Others are concerned with problems from greasy fumes. But let's face it, if you've been heating with wood or coal at least one season, you already know that the curtains need to be laundered an extra time or two each year and that the walls, ceiling, and woodwork require a little extra attention. So if you're going to be doing the extra work anyway, you might just as well take advantage of the heat and put it to practical use.

HINTS: A small fan placed behind heaters without circulators does a good job of circulating heat to all areas of the house, and it costs only pennies a day to run.

Regulating the Heat

Many foods such as soups, stews, sauces, and pot roast can be cooked for a long time over low heat or for shorter periods at higher temperatures. Many casseroles and even roasts can be included in this category, so your stovetop temperature is not as critical when cooking these foods slowly as long as you've got plenty of time and don't mind watching the pot. Other foods such as breads, cakes, cheese and egg dishes must be cooked quickly at higher temperatures, and you must watch your stovetop thermometer carefully to cook them successfully.

There is such a variety of wood and coal heaters that I will not even attempt to suggest how to run your particular stove, but here are some general principles for effective stove operation during the cooking processes called for in the recipes in this book.

The factor crucial to the success of this type of cooking is the temperature of the pan and not the source of heat, so you need a good hot fire that is going to remain fairly stable throughout the cooking period. This is true of charcoal and open fires too. Stovetop burners on gas, oil, and electric stoves are the easiest to regulate, since all you have to do is adjust the burner.

Unless you start off with a good bed of hot coals as a base, you will have to add wood or coal often, and each time you do, the temperature in your cooking unit will drop until the new material becomes combustible. So **be sure to have your fire started well ahead of cooking time and then add small amounts of wood or coal periodically.** This will keep the temperature fairly stable.

Building a Quick Hot Fire

On some days that are not cold enough to keep your wood or coal heater going full blast, you may need high temperatures for a short time in order to cook or bake a particular dish. This is when dry softwood is very valuable. It ignites quickly, burns hot, and dies down as soon as you stop feeding the softwood to the stove.

On these warmer days, it is more difficult to bake breads, cakes, and pies on top-loading woodstoves than on front- or side-loaders, because frequent feeding of softwood into the stove would require removing the pan from the stove surface, thus disturbing the crucial baking process. But while breads, cakes, and pies require fairly hot baking temperatures during the first part of the baking time in order to rise well or set a crust, the baking time is quite short. On relatively warm days, place the cast-iron oven on the stove early to preheat slowly. That done, you need to build a quick hot fire only when it's time for the critical period of baking. Add to the stove a few chunks of softwood that are just 3–4 inches in diameter. To the top of the softwood, add another 3–4 chunks of well-seasoned hardwood of the same size. This will effectively raise your temperature fast and keep it up long enough to achieve the desired results. After that, if the temperature falls back slightly, it won't endanger the ultimate success of the recipe. Don't be afraid to run your stove hot a couple of times a day. It is recommended that you do just this in order to prevent creosote build-up. Time these hot periods to coincide with your cooking. This is an ideal time to bake items that require high baking temperatures.

Since I do not own a coal stove, I went to one of the dealers in our area and asked his opinion on how to get a quick hot fire with coal. He suggested adding charcoal.

Stove Too Hot?

Occasionally your heat source will get too hot, and you must correct the situation immediately. **When you can't reduce the temperature of the heat source, then you must change the position of your cast-iron oven.** On a charcoal grill, raise the grill or lower the coals. If your grill isn't adjustable, place 2 large flat stones or bricks on the grill about 8 inches apart. Place a heavy rack across these stones and put your cast-iron oven on the rack. If you are cooking over an open fire, raise your oven.

Space bricks 8 inches apart, add cake rack, then cast-iron oven to reduce baking temperature in oven quickly when heat source becomes too hot.

On a wood or coal stove, the same effect can be produced by placing the cast-iron oven on a **low metal rack or trivet,** which separates the oven from the heat source enough to lower the cooking temperature, even though the actual temperature of the stove surface remains high. This is a useful technique, too, for the times when you have adjusted the woodstove to reduce its temperature, but the stove takes some time to respond to being turned down; in the interim, a trivet or metal rack may prevent burned food.

Adding Wood or Coal to Top-Loaders

There will be times when you are cooking a dish that takes a long time, such as a large roast, a stew, or soup, on a top-loading stove, and you will need to replenish your wood or coal supply. Plan ahead for these times so that you will not lose precious heat and ultimately extend your cooking time. Draw a small table or chair up close to the stove and place an old blanket on it. Get the wood you are going to add right down in front of the stove before you move the cast-iron oven. Open the damper on the stove, remove the oven quickly, and set it down on the blanket-covered table. Bring the blanket up over the oven. Add the wood to the stove quickly, move the oven back to the stove immediately, and then readjust the dampers as necessary. (Never use this method for baked products as the shifting of the cast-iron oven would cause the cake or bread to fall.)

Open-Fire Cooking

The best way to cook over an open fire is to construct a tripod, using three pieces of metal pipe. Drill holes in one end of the pipe and thread a long, heavy bolt through the pipes and a small chain, positioning the chain ends to either side of the center pipe, as in the sketch. Use S hooks to hold your oven at the height you need to obtain proper cooking temperatures. This kind of cooking outdoors can be quite a challenge and lots of fun.

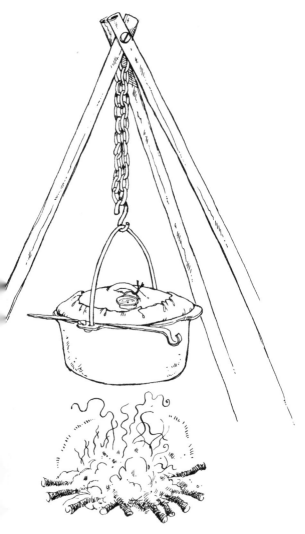

Adjust cooking temperature by moving S hook holding cast-iron oven up or down on chain.

Equipment for Stovetop Baking

The soups, stews, and fried foods in this cookbook can be prepared on any stovetop using ordinary pans, but baked items require a special kind of pan. This doesn't necessarily mean that you must buy another pan, because many homes already have a **cast-iron Dutch oven with an iron cover** or the popular enamel-coated cast-iron Dutch ovens. If you do not own a cast-iron Dutch oven and must buy one, I would suggest that you purchase an 8-quart size with an *iron* cover, since you can cook an entire meal in this or larger sizes.

No other type of pan except possibly the heaviest type of cast aluminum will do for this kind of baking. If you have cast aluminum on hand, you might want to try it out before you invest in a cast-iron pan. (See temperature-control testing, p. 14.) I do recommend an agateware (porcelain on steel) roaster for some items, but it is too lightweight to be used except for large roasts or turkeys.

When you are working with a wood or coal stove that is hot enough for frying, you can be pretty sure it is uncomfortably warm near the stove, so you really need long-handled wooden spoons as well as long-handled spatulas and meat forks. Barbecue equipment works well.

Along with the 4–8-quart cast-iron Dutch oven, the items listed below are important for this type of baking. Many of these items can already be found in your cupboards.

Spatter screen
Timer
Heavy metal trivets (preferably cast-iron) with little feet
Thermometers (meat, deep-fat, dairy, candy)
All sizes of round Pyrex and black steel baking dishes
6-cup gelatin mold
Heavy-duty tinfoil
Empty, clean tuna-fish cans (to be used to bake in or to raise baking rack)
Cake-cooling racks
1 large roaster (cast-iron or agateware (porcelain on steel)) with cover
1 large tin-can lid
Racks that will fit inside cast-iron Dutch oven and roaster. The racks should stand at least ¾ inch off the bottom of the pan.
2 long shish kebab skewers (2 teaspoons can be used but are not as good)
1 oven thermometer

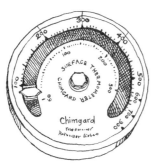

Stovestack thermometer

Stovetop thermometer

Oven thermometer

2 stovetop thermometers
1 stovestack thermometer (for wood- and coal-heater owners only)
Long-handled spoons, spatulas, and meat forks, cotton gardening gloves (see p. 24)

Stovetop and stovestack thermometers differ from one another and from oven thermometers and should not be used interchangeably. Each is designed for a specific purpose, and the temperature sensors work properly only when used to indicate the types of heat they are designed for. **Stovetop thermometers** are designed to tell you the temperature of your cooking surface; most **stovestack thermometers** are designed to tell you the temperature of your stovepipe. Each of these thermometers registers accurately only when in contact with the proper hot surface. **Oven thermometers** are designed to give the temperature of the space within a confined area, i.e. an oven, broiler, or a covered cooking vessel. Stovetop and stovestack thermometers are available at wood and coal stove stores, as well as some hardware stores. Oven thermometers are available wherever cooking utensils are sold. Those who will be cooking on gas, electric, or oil burners need purchase only one stovetop thermometer.

I use a stovestack thermometer for two reasons. First, I can tell when my stove is getting dangerously hot, and second, I don't have to stand over my oven to know when the temperature is dropping: when the temperature on the stack thermometer falls, I can see it from across the room.

Use common sense when selecting **baking dishes** for this type of oven. They must fit in the cast-iron Dutch oven with a space of at least ¾ inch, all the way around, between the baking dish and the wall of the oven. Everything cooks faster and more evenly in the larger-diameter, straight-sided, low-baking dishes. It is very important to use the right size baking dish: casseroles or cake batters should fill the dish at least two-thirds full for a good-quality finished product. The diameter of the baking dish is not as important for roasts. Dense items such as meat loaves, cakes, etc., bake well and in less time in tube pans.

Tin or aluminum bakeware can be used for meat loaves and casseroles, but it is more subject to hot spots; therefore some areas might burn before baked products such as cakes or rolls are done throughout. I personally **prefer Pyrex baking dishes or black steel.** Both conduct heat evenly at lower temperatures and give nice brown bottom crusts. Many of us have one or two of these black steel heavy-duty 1–2-quart saucepans with removable handles for general cooking, but we seldom think to remove the handles because there isn't any real reason to do so. Using these would save the cost of new baking dishes.

Care of Cast Iron

If you take good care of your cast-iron Dutch oven, it will last you a lifetime. When new, it should be **seasoned by coating it with fat and heating it over medium heat for at least 2 hours.** Cool and wipe dry. If your oven gives off a metallic taste, it's because it wasn't seasoned properly, or because it needs to be reseasoned. Sometimes it has to be done 3 or 4 times at first. Wash your oven and the inside of your foil-lined cover after each use with warm sudsy water; rinse and dry thoroughly. Do not use abrasive pads or cleansers. Wipe the inside of the dry cast-iron oven with a lightly oiled cloth or paper towel before storing. To prevent rusting, never store the cast-iron oven with the cover on tightly.

As with your regular oven, you will sometimes have spills that burn onto the bottom of your cast-iron oven. Scour thoroughly, using an abrasive pad if necessary, and reseason. Always rinse the cast-iron oven with warm water and wipe dry before using it to bake; otherwise the protective oil will smoke as the oven heats.

Preparing the Cast-Iron Oven for Baking

Prepare your oven in the following manner: **Place a round wire cake rack in the bottom of your cast-iron Dutch oven.** It should stand at least ¾ inch off the bottom of the pan so the heat can circulate properly. (Screw-bands from canning jars can be used to lift the rack to the proper level.) **Line the cover with enough heavy-duty tinfoil to come up over the cover of the pan on the outside** about 1 inch all around. If you are careful when you handle the foil, it will last a long time.

PREPARING CAST-IRON OVEN FOR BAKING AND TESTING.

Wire cake rack, supported by canning screw-bands if necessary to achieve ¾- to 1- inch space between bottom of oven and rack.

Cover inside of lid with heavy-duty tinfoil. Bring foil up over outside of cover at least 1 inch.

Pot ready to bake.

Cutaway view of proper rack positioning.

Venting

The cast-iron oven should be **vented by placing long shish kebab skewers in the positions noted in the sketches.** Slip the end of the skewer under the bail handle of the Dutch oven to prevent it from falling if you move the cover to check the progress of your recipe. Sketch 1 indicates the proper placement of one skewer for light venting. This is called **position 1.** There should be exactly ⅛ inch between cover and pan. Sketch 2 indicates proper placement of 2 skewers, placed in the same position as position 1, when more venting is needed for such items as cakes, breads, and soufflés, or to brown casserole toppings. In this position there should be ⅛ inch **between the cover and pan on both sides.** This is called **position 2.** Sketch 3 indicates proper placement of the skewers when you need lower temperatures toward the end of a cooking procedure or when you are cooling cream puffs or meringues in the oven off the heat. This is called **position 3.**

It is very important that you learn to vent the oven properly. Too much venting will drastically reduce the temperature inside your oven. Remember, you are using cast iron; once the iron cover has heated to a temperature of 175°F on your stovetop thermometer, you should have an inside temperature of at least 400°F. But if the oven is vented too much, the cast iron might still register 175°F outside, but the temperature inside would be too low for baking properly.

Adapting Venting to Your Own Recipes

To adapt venting to your recipes: **venting position 1 is used in all general baking** when an average amount of moisture release is adequate. This includes casseroles and early stages of pies where hot temperatures to set crusts are important. It is the hottest method of baking, with the smallest release of moisture.

Venting position 2 is used when you need even rising of baked products, such as breads, brownies, cakes, etc. Position 2 may also be used to roast meat and to release extra moisture. It is the best position for the last half of the baking time for casseroles and pies that need extra browning. Temperatures in position 2 are moderate.

Venting position 3 is used when lower temperatures are needed for slow browning and for recipes that need extra moisture released toward the end of the cooking period.

VENTING POSITION 1.

Tuck one long skewer under bail handle between lip of cover and pan. Lid should be raised ⅛ inch.

"You will not be able to see inside of pan; note position of inner lip of cover."

VENTING POSITION 2.

Place skewers on both sides of cast-iron oven between *lip of cover* and pan. Space should be ⅛ inch between cover and lid all around the pan.

"Note position of inner lip of cover."

VENTING POSITION 3.

Move skewers 1½ - 2 inches toward center of cast-iron oven. Lid is now raised ⅜ inch all around the pan.

"It is now possible to see into top of pan just a little."

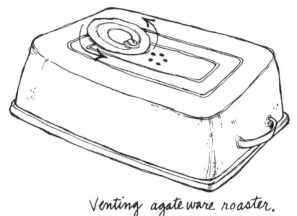

Venting agateware roaster.

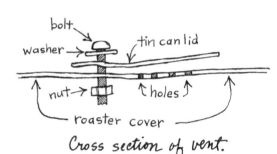

bolt

washer→

tin can lid

nut→ ↑holes↑

— roaster cover —

Cross section of vent.

This position is also useful when the temperature of your heating unit gets too high; the temperature within your cast-iron oven remains much lower with venting in this position. With just a little experience, you will be able to adjust the venting to your recipes without any trouble at all.

Preparing the Agateware Roaster for Baking

Drill five ⅝–½-inch holes in the center of the roaster cover as in the sketch. To the left of these and through a tin-can lid large enough to cover all holes, drill another hole (½ inch from the edge of the can lid). Make sure to smooth down the rough edges of the holes on the underside of the roaster cover to prevent injury when washing the pan. Thread a small bolt with a washer and a nut through the can lid and the roaster top as in the sketch. Now the can lid will slide back and forth over the vent holes of the roaster to either keep moisture in or let it out. Lightweight aluminum roasters should not be used for this type of baking as they heat too quickly, and food would burn on the outside before it would cook through.

Putting it All Together: Baking Principles

The method involved in this kind of baking is very simple. **The cast-iron Dutch oven is prepared as above, the baking dish is placed on the rack, and the skewer is placed between the pan and the foil-lined cover to vent moisture.** Now you have a miniature oven that works just like a standard oven. You are baking with dry heat that circulates freely around your baking dish. Moisture from the cooking food is vented between the pan and cover by means of the skewer (see sketch). You do not get as much browning on the top of baked goods such as breads and rolls as you would in a standard oven, but sides and bottom crusts are beautifully browned.

Temperature Control

Unlike a standard oven, your cast-iron oven does not have a thermostat that automatically shuts off the heating unit when your oven gets too hot or turns the unit back on when the temperature drops too low, so you must learn the art of temperature control. This is very easy, but it does take a few

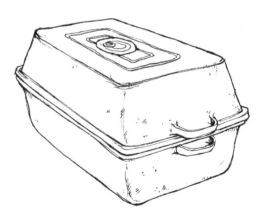

Roaster ready to bake.

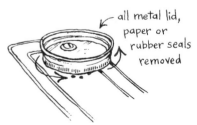

all metal lid, paper or rubber seals removed

Wide-mouth Mason jar cover may be used instead of tin can lid.

hours of your time. These hours will pay off in energy savings for years to come.

Every stove works a little differently. This is true of different types and sizes of cookware too. So it pays to take a day to establish some definite guidelines for your particular situation. Make sure that you have at least half a day to do some testing. Making the charts described below will tell you the exact relationship, *for your stove,* between (a) stove surface temperature, (b) baking temperature (inside the pan), and (c) pan-top temperature. This will pay off in perfect results with your recipes every time. If you are an avid camper, it's worth a bag of charcoal to do temperature-control testing on your grill.

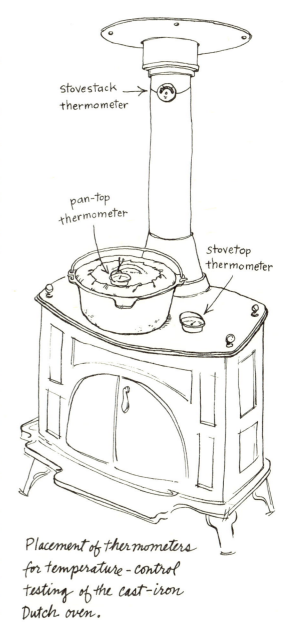

Placement of thermometers for temperature-control testing of the cast-iron Dutch oven.

Making a Temperature Chart for your Own Stove

(Steps 1–3 for wood and coal heaters only)

1. Fire up your stove and establish a good steady fire. If the stove has been going for some time, make sure that ashes haven't built up too much (this would distort your temperature findings), then establish a good bed of coals before beginning your temperature testing.

2. Place **stovestack** thermometer at the highest point on the stovepipe (between the stove and the first partition it must pass through; see sketch). Put it where it can be easily seen.

3. Place **stovetop** thermometer directly on the cooking surface. (If you are not using a wood or coal heater, omit steps #1–3 and start with step #4.)

4. Place your **cast-iron Dutch oven** on the stovetop. Place the **cake rack** in the bottom and put an **oven thermometer** on the rack, positioning it carefully so that you can check it quickly by just barely raising the edge of the cover (see sketch). If the

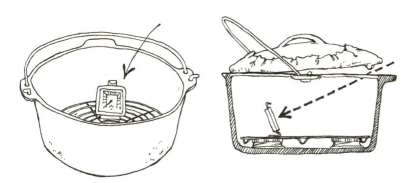

Placement of oven thermometer inside oven so it can be seen without taking cover off oven.

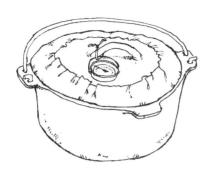

Placement of pan-top thermometer on lid of cast-iron oven. To be used for temperature-control testing and for all cooking with cast-iron oven. With short piece of wire secure pan-top thermometer to lid handle.

A Reminder: Even if a recipe calls for a baking temperature of 375°F, you can bake it at lower temperatures, in most instances, just by baking it longer.

HINTS: When I know I am going to be using my cast-iron oven for baking during the day, I put it on the woodstove early in the morning so it's ready when I need it. If it's a particularly cold day and you are running your stove at its maximum heating capacity, you could place your oven on a trivet to prevent it from becoming overheated, or you could keep the cover off.

oven thermometer is not easy to see with a quick peek, the heat loss caused by fully raising or removing the lid will affect the accuracy of all the temperature readings on your chart.

5. Prepare your cover as directed (See p. 11) and put the cover on the pan so it fits snugly.

6. Place **stovetop** thermometer on the cover of the Dutch oven, as close to the center as possible, and secure with wire to the lid-handle. Start preheating your oven.

7. Start your chart by checking all the temperatures (of the 4 thermometers) with the cast-iron oven unvented. Some recipes, including all that call for a "covered casserole," require unvented cooking, so be sure to include this part of the testing.

8. After checking temperatures in the unvented position, remove Dutch oven from stove and let it cool. When the cast iron has cooled, test the oven *vented* in *position 2*. You can safely assume that **temperatures in position 1 will be approximately 25 degrees higher and temperatures in position 3 will be approximately 25 degrees lower.**

9. Follow the same procedure for testing your roaster.

10. Use the following charts for your testing. They will be your personal temperature-control guide.

11. Filling in the chart: as the *pan-top* temperature starts to rise, record all the correlating temperatures (of all 4 thermometers) on the chart. Begin when the pan-top temperature reaches 100°F. Go on to record each of the next temperature settings on the chart. **By the time your cast-iron oven *pan-top* temperature reaches 175°F, you will undoubtedly have a *stovestack* temperature of about 360°F and a *stovetop* temperature of 500–600°F.** This sounds very high, but these are probably the temperatures you have been heating with on very cold days without realizing it. They are the uppermost temperature limits for the safe operation of your stove. Many types of stoves will have to operate at lower *stovetop* temperatures in order to keep the stovepipe (*stovestack*) temperatures within the safety zone. *You can still bake successfully as long as you have a stovetop temperature of at least 450°F.* (This is a baking temperature of 300°F in my cast-iron oven on my woodstove.) You will just have to bake longer. When a recipe calls for a "baking" temperature of 325–350°F, you should be able to tell from your own chart just exactly what *pan-top* temperatures your little pan-top thermometer should register. Temperatures will be approximate and will vary slightly, but they will be close enough to give accurate results. Remember, our grandmothers did it without the help of thermometers.

CAST-IRON OVEN UNVENTED

Pan-top Temperature	Stovestack Temperature	Stovetop Temperature	Baking *(inside the pan)* Temperature
100°F			
125°F			
150°F			
175°F			

CAST-IRON OVEN VENTED (in position 2)

Pan-Top Temperature	Stovestack Temperature	Stovetop Temperature	Baking Temperature
100°F			
125°F			
150°F			
175°F			

ROASTER UNVENTED

Pan-Top Temperature	Stovestack Temperature	Stovetop Temperature	Baking Temperature
100°F			
125°F			
150°F			
175°F			

ROASTER VENTED

Pan-Top Temperature	Stovestack Temperature	Stovetop Temperature	Baking Temperature
100°F			
125°F			
150°F			
175°F			

Testing My Dutch Oven

The figures in the sample chart below are for a vented 8-quart cast-iron Dutch oven on my woodstove. These figures are included *only* to show an *example* of how a chart looks when completed; the figures themselves are not to be considered "normative." **Every stove works differently, and you must ascertain the temperatures for your own stove.**

CAST-IRON OVEN **VENTED** IN POSITION 2

Pan-Top Temperature	Stovestack Temperature	Stovetop Temperature	Baking (inside the pan) Temperature
100°F	270°F	450°F	230–300°F*
125°F	290°F	550°F	325°F
150°F	360°F	600°F	390°F
175°F	360°F	625°F	435°F

*Varies with length of time on stovetop at 450°F.

These are the maximum temperatures that I can achieve on my woodstove. Gas and electric as well as oil stovetop burners can achieve higher temperatures, but they would cause burning on the bottom of baked items.

Roaster bottom with rack in place supported by tuna cans. Thermometer ready for temperature-control test.

Preheating

It takes about **30 minutes to preheat an 8-quart cast-iron Dutch oven on my woodstove to a baking temperature of 350°F,** if I start it on a stove that has a stovetop temperature of 450°F. While this may seem slow, you must remember that it is this very factor that makes cast iron so effective for this type of baking. It does not fluctuate rapidly in temperature. Once heated, it will maintain for a long time the stable baking temperature you want.

It takes approximately 15 minutes to preheat the same size pan on my gas range with the burner set on high. (If you are in a hurry, you might want to preheat your cast-iron oven on your gas, electric, or oil stove before baking on the wood or coal heater.) Once heated, it will maintain a baking temperature of 350°F on the lowest flame I can get on my gas burner.

Testing the Roaster Oven

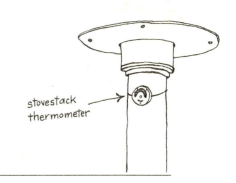

stovestack thermometer

Test your roaster for temperature control the same way you tested your cast-iron Dutch oven. The following is an example of my test. (The figures are *not* to be considered normative for other stoves.)

ROASTER VENTED

Pan-Top Temperature	Stovestack Temperature	Stovetop Temperature	Baking Temperature
150°F	250°F	450°F	225°F
175°F	275°F	450°F	275°F
200°F	280°F	500°F	325°F

You will notice several differences between the roaster and the cast-iron Dutch oven. The roaster will heat faster (it will also cool very quickly). You need higher *pan-top* temperatures on the roaster to achieve the same baking temperature as with the cast iron. If you set your rack at different heights within the roaster, you will find that the temperatures vary considerably: very hot on the bottom, cooler toward the top. In order to prevent the roaster temperature from rising further than you want, you must adjust the dampers often. So what's the roaster good for? If you don't mind watching the pot a little more, it does a good job of roasting a turkey. In fact, you can roast the turkey, stuffing, vegetables and potatoes, then make the gravy, all in one pan (see Roast Turkey Dinner, p. 94). This not only saves the energy you would have used in the oven and several stovetop burners, it saves cleanup time and hot water later.

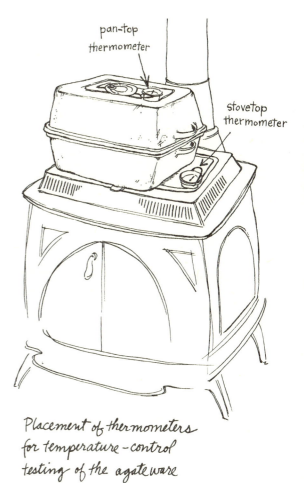

pan-top thermometer

stovetop thermometer

Placement of thermometers for temperature-control testing of the agateware roaster.

Keeping Foods Warm Until Serving Time

Occasionally when you are serving several people, or more than one dish, it will be important to keep something such as a roast warm while preparing mashed potatoes. If you live in a house with a well-equipped kitchen, this wouldn't seem to present a problem. But it would be a shame to save energy cooking foods only to waste it keeping the foods warm, so I have a few suggestions.

We'll start with the more expensive ideas and go down to

free methods. First of all there is the **Crock-Pot.** Since it costs only a few cents to run for several hours, and it has many other uses, it is definitely a wise investment. **Warming trays** do a good job, as do large wide-mouth **thermos jugs (for gravies and sauces), double boilers** with boiling water in the bottom, or even a pan or bowl larger than the cooking dish that will hold boiling water around your hot dish. Cover your dish with a heavy towel to keep the heat in.

Bricks do a good job of retaining heat for a long time. Heat them on the top of your wood or coal heater or right on the top of the cast-iron oven, then place them in a small box with your cooking pan on the top and cover with a heavy towel. Remember this when you're camping and always keep bricks or large flat stones on fires you light for cooking or heat, to keep food or water hot for a long time after meals.

A small broiler can be used to brown the tops of casseroles or crisp the skin on small poultry, if these touches are very important to you. If you're roasting a turkey the energy-saving way, you have saved so much energy that you could finish browning the skin until crisp, about 30 minutes, in your stove oven. Properly used, your little cast-iron oven will do a pretty good job of browning most products.

How to Use the Recipes in This Cookbook

Most of these recipes are economical, high-protein main dishes that make a meal by themselves or complete meals that can be cooked all at the same time in the cast-iron Dutch oven or roaster. These foods need only a salad, bread, beverage, and dessert to complete the meal. I have included other recipes for homemade mixes and sauces and desserts that are good, easy, and inexpensive to prepare. Many more home-made mixes are in my book *How to Live on Almost Nothing and Have Plenty,* published by Alfred A. Knopf (1979).

Don't be afraid to experiment with your own recipes (see p. 25). Once you learn the basic principles of this kind of cooking, you can cook anything. If my recipes are too large for your family, you may halve or even quarter the recipes quite successfully, with the exception of breads and desserts. Adjust the seasonings carefully and be sure not to cook the foods as long as you would the larger amount.

All of my recipes require a minimum of preparation. You do not need to live in the kitchen to be a good cook. Spending an occasional day or just odd bits of time here and there, doing such things as dicing onion, pepper, and celery for casseroles and soups and tossing them in the freezer, or making up sauces and soup stocks and crumbing bread and crackers for stuffing and toppings, helps to make daily food preparation less time-consuming and more economical as well, because it allows you to put many leftovers to good use.

Here are some of the ingredients called for in recipes and what you can use as substitutes. For instance, you might want to try a recipe that you've found in a magazine that calls for canned soup. There are many homemade soup purées and simple sauces that you can make or have on hand that are just as good, if not better.

I USE	YOU MAY SUBSTITUTE
¾ cup honey with a pinch of baking soda (and bake a little longer)	1 cup sugar
¾ tablespoon honey	1 tablespoon sugar
1 cup firmly packed brown sugar *or* 1 cup molasses and ½ teaspoon soda, less ¼ cup liquid in the recipe *or* 1½ cups maple syrup less ½ cup liquid in the recipe	1 cup granulated sugar
1 cup cream	1 cup whole milk with ⅓ cup powdered dry milk and 1 tablespoon butter or margarine *or* 1 cup double-strength reconstituted dry milk with 1 tablespoon butter *or* 1 cup of evaporated milk
1 cup rich broth	1 cup water with 2 packages powdered bouillon or 2 bouillon cubes (and reduce salt in recipe by 1 teaspoon)
1¼ cups homemade puréed soup with 1 tablespoon flour if purée is not thick enough	1 can condensed soup
1 cup sour cream	1 cup yogurt
8 ounces cream cheese	1½ cups large-curd cottage cheese well drained, with as much moisture pressed out as possible.

Pork drippings (bacon, lard, ham, or pork roast)	Butter, margarine, salad oil
Butter (Do keep one stick of real butter on hand for special dishes. It adds so much to the flavor.)	Margarine
1 ounce unsweetened chocolate	3 tablespoons unsweetened bakers' cocoa or carob powder with 1 tablespoon fat
1 ounce semisweet chocolate	1 ounce chocolate chips
¾ cup plus 2 tablespoons all-purpose flour with 1 tablespoon cornstarch	1 cup cake flour
Shrimp, crabmeat, lobster	Canned shellfish
1 cup tomato sauce	1 cup commercial tomato sauce *or* 2 cups tomato juice reduced by half
1 cup sour milk or buttermilk	Scant 1 cup whole sweet milk with 1 tablespoon lemon juice or vinegar
1 cup fish stock	1 cup clam juice
1 egg	2 egg yolks
1 tablespoon flour for thickening	½ tablespoon cornstarch *or* 2 tablespoons quick-cooking tapioca *or* 1 tablespoon granular tapioca *or* 2 tablespoons granular cereal
1 tablespoon fresh chopped herbs	1 teaspoon dried herbs

The Paper Towel Method

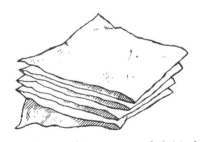

8 sheets of paper towel folded into the size of one sheet.

As I stated earlier, I love a challenge, and baking quick breads and cakes in a cast-iron oven was a *real* challenge; batters are moist and heavy, and the oven's small size doesn't leave much room for the amount of hot, dry air needed to absorb all that extra moisture quickly so that these breads and cakes can rise successfully. Additional venting could be helpful, but that would reduce the temperature within the oven to the point that rapid rising couldn't take place.

One day while cooking potatoes, I put the cover of the pan down on the counter top to test for doneness. When I returned the cover to the pan, I unconsciously grabbed for a piece of paper towel to wipe up the condensation that had formed on the counter top under the hot cover. Standing there with the paper towel in my hand, it occurred to me that I might have the answer to my dilemma.

I couldn't just put the paper towels over the baking dish because they would fall in and stick to the batter; besides, they needed to be held high enough to allow the cake to rise. In the end, I decided on a piece of chicken wire. It could be molded over any dish, dome shaped, and would hold the paper towels nicely. I tried it, and it worked beautifully.

When a recipe in this book states that it should be baked with paper towels, you should arrange the towels in the following manner: take 8 sheets of paper towel and fold them to the size of 1 towel. Mold a 12-inch square of 1-inch chicken wire to fit over your baking dish. Place the towels on top of the wire and tuck the 4 corners into the wire (see sketches). These paper towels can be reused since they do not retain the flavor of the foods being baked.

Rules for Stovetop Cooking

Though I will refer to the following steps throughout the book, it is sometimes helpful to have them all together in one section for quick reference.

All degrees are given in the Fahrenheit and U.S. Customary System, but the conversion chart for Metric and Celsius is on page 27.

If your recipe says to preheat the oven, then your cast-iron Dutch oven should be preheated until the baking temperature on the pan-top thermometer indicates that according to *your* charts the required (*baking*) temperature inside the cast-iron oven has been reached.

Buy a meat thermometer with a short shank (about 3 inches long). Instead of putting the thermometer into the meat on the top, place it in the center of the meat through the side of the roast. (Placement for turkey will be shown in the sketch on p. 95.)

When a recipe calls for a covered casserole, simply place your uncovered casserole in the Dutch oven and put the cast-iron cover on without venting.

For a nice brown appearance, brown meats in hot fat on all sides prior to roasting.

When first placing a solid piece of meat or most casseroles in the cast-iron oven, bake, unvented, for 20 minutes to recover heat loss quickly. After basting, roast, unvented, for 5–10 minutes.

Chicken wire molded to fit top of glass baking dish.

Paper towels secured by tucking corners into holes in chicken wire.

Put baking dish with paper towel cover in Dutch oven.

Covered baking dish on cake rack inside Dutch oven with lid vented.

To reduce cooking time for casseroles, heat the soup purées, sauces, or liquids called for in the recipe on the stove surface (whenever possible) before adding them to the dish.

Set your timer! It's very easy to get busy and forget to check the time on recipes. Opening the oven too soon could ruin your baked goods.

Don't peek until 80 per cent of the cooking time is up. Then crack the cover quickly to see if the recipe has cooked enough to be tested. The reason for this is that as soon as the cover is removed, heat rises quickly, and if a cake or bread isn't done enough, it won't be able to recover from the shock of change in temperature and will fall.

If your stove surface is uneven, use a table knife or other small object to level the rack *within* your cast-iron oven.

Wear a pair of cotton gardening gloves to prevent burns to the back of your hands when removing baking dishes from the hot cast-iron oven.

When trying new recipes, follow the timing given in the recipe. Don't peek until the full time is up, and you'll find that you have fewer failures.

If a recipe such as those for cream puffs or meringues says to cool in the oven, remove the cast-iron oven from the heat and vent by placing both skewers in position 3. This raises the entire cover just enough.

If you substitute honey for sugar in any of your recipes, be sure to bake a little bit longer. If you substitute sugar for honey in any of my recipes, check them 10 minutes sooner than the time suggested.

General Cooking Suggestions

Use stable products to prevent failures. Those I consider most stable are gluten flour (available at health food stores) for baked goods, Red Star yeast, and King Arthur all-purpose unbleached flour. I have tried all the popular brands of flour, and though this flour is more expensive, I like it best. I'm sure this is because it is higher in gluten than other flour. If you are not able to find it in your area, or you would rather not change from the brand you are using, I suggest that you add 1 tablespoon of gluten flour to every cup of all-purpose flour you use.

The new spray-on vegetable oil coatings are better than greasing and flouring your baking dishes for baked goods; sometimes the flour on the bottom of the dish will burn.

Placement of meat thermometer in small roast. If thermometer is stuck straight down into top of roast, the lid may not fit over the roast, especially in a cast-iron Dutch oven.

When blending hot liquids, never fill the blender or food processor container more than half way, or you could get burned.

Never boil soups that contain cream. After adding cream, heat just to the point where soup is piping hot.

Many of the recipes in this book can be cooked in a Crock-Pot. Adjust the cooking time according to the instructions that come with your Crock-Pot and don't use quite as much seasoning or the full amount of water called for in the recipe, since flavorings are stronger in Crock-Pot cooking and there is no evaporation of liquids.

Adapting Your Own Recipes

If your recipes call for an oven temperature higher than you can achieve within your cast-iron oven, you know you must bake longer. If your recipe calls for a preheated oven, then preheat your cast-iron oven on the stove, with the cover on tightly. Place your baking dish in the oven quickly, so as not to lose heat, and follow the directions for venting (p. 12). Always bake the full time given in your recipe before checking; this will eliminate fallen cakes and breads. Usually you will find that you must bake just a little bit longer. Always note baking temperature and timing on your recipes for future reference.

I accidentally found a way to test new recipes for doneness: follow your nose! Recently, when I was testing a new cake, someone shut off my timer by mistake. I wasn't sure when I had put the cake in, so I was really worried, until I found it was beginning to smell done. I checked, and sure enough, it was. Later, I tried this test on other baked products and found it to be reasonably accurate.

Baking at Lower Temperatures

Many days it isn't cold enough to run your heater at maximum temperatures. But breads, rolls, and even cakes can be baked at temperatures as much as 75 degrees lower than a recipe recommends. Certain rules, however, must be observed. Have your fire hot enough to preheat the cast-iron oven to a baking temperature of 350–375°F. *Check your own temperature-control charts.* Keep the heat up the first 15–20 minutes of baking time, then let it fall gradually, but never lower than a setting that correlates with a baking temperature of 300°F on your pan-top thermometer. Bake about one-third longer than the recommended time before checking. (See p. 7 on how to build a quick hot fire.)

Cake rack supported by screw-bands from canning-jar lids to get proper space between rack and bottom of Dutch oven.

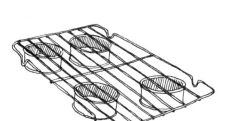

Cake rack for agateware roaster supported by tuna-fish cans.

Trouble Shooting

Something went wrong! Your cake fell or the roast didn't cook, and you don't know why. Here are some questions you should ask yourself:

1. Did you use a stovetop thermometer to check the temperature of your cast-iron oven or did you just "think" it was hot enough?

2. Was the baking dish the size called for in the recipe?

3. Is your cast-iron oven much larger or smaller than my 8-quart one? If so, you should test it for temperature control (see p. 17).

4. Did you follow the recipe instructions carefully?

5. Your cake fell, or it rose and then collapsed. Did you vent the cast-iron oven enough to allow steam to escape? Did you vent it too much, losing too much heat? See venting instructions, page 12.

6. Your baked product was too dry on the sides and bottom. Was the temperature of the heat source too high? Was the baking rack too low? The rack could be raised slightly by using tuna cans or canning-jar screw-bands. A more shallow dish would allow the center of the baked product to bake in the same length of time as the edges, making it evenly moist throughout.

7. Your bread failed to rise. Was your yeast fresh? Had it been kept for several days in an area that was too warm? Was it warmed to room temperature before using if it had been refrigerated? Yeast should be stored in a cool place and brought to room temperature before using. Do not place your breads in the preheated cast-iron oven until they have risen to double in bulk. Did you start with your heat too low? Did you vent enough? It might be necessary, especially if you're adapting your own recipe, to try the Paper Towel Method (p. 22).

8. Your roast cooked too slowly. Was your heat source too low? Did you vent too much? Recheck temperature control.

9. Your roast cooked too quickly. Was your heat source too high? You might use a trivet under your roaster. Did you vent enough? Recheck temperature control.

Often a simple adjustment is the answer, and the more you cook this way, the more proficient you will become in adapting your own recipes to this energy-saving way of cooking. Don't be afraid to experiment.

Make Your Own Notes

All of these recipes were tested on my woodstove and gas range, and many of them on a charcoal grill. They were very successful, but everyone handles his or her work a little differently, so we've left a space called "COOK'S NOTES" at the end of each recipe. When you try a recipe for the first time, follow my directions carefully and you can't come out far from wrong. But your stove may need a little longer or shorter baking time, you may have to make adjustments in your venting or temperature, or you may use a different size pan or baking dish. Make sure to include all this information in your COOK'S NOTES so that the next time you try the recipe it will come out just right.

I have saved this final remark until last, before you go on to the recipe section:

Read all recipes at least twice before starting, to be sure you understand them and have all the equipment and ingredients required!

FAHRENHEIT DEGREES	CELSIUS DEGREES	U.S. CUSTOMARY SYSTEM	METRIC SYSTEM	
0	−18	⅕ teaspoon	1	milliliter
40	4	1 teaspoon	5	milliliters
137	58	1 tablespoon	15	milliliters
140	60	⅕ cup	50	milliliters
160	70	1 cup	240	milliliters
170	75	2 cups (1 pint)	470	milliliters
300	150	4 cups (1 quart)	.95	liter
325	165	4 quarts (1 gallon)	3.8	liters
350	175	1 fluid ounce	30	milliliters or 28 grams
375	190	1 pound	454	grams

THE RECIPES

Please Read the Preceding Chapter Thoroughly
Before Attempting to Use the Recipes in This Cookbook

Basics (Items called for in other recipes throughout the book)

Beef Stock

ABOUT 4 QUARTS

Good beef stock can be made from just beef bones and 3–4 pounds of plate or shin beef, but to save money it would be wiser to set aside not only bones but also trimmings and leftovers from any cut of beef. When you have 4–5 pounds of trimmings tucked away in the freezer (see HINTS), put the soup kettle on the heater and brew up a pot of rich beef stock.

1 medium-sized piece suet, cubed
2 large carrots, scraped and chopped coarse
1 large onion, chopped
1 cup chopped celery leaves and tops
1 small white turnip, chopped
4 pounds plate or shin beef or beef leftovers and trimmings
4–5 pounds beef bones (add veal bones if you have any)
2 tablespoons Worcestershire sauce
1 tablespoon salt
¼ teaspoon pepper
½ teaspoon powdered cloves

In a large, heavy soup kettle, render pieces of suet until almost all fat has melted. Add vegetables to pot and sauté until onions are limp but not brown. Add remaining ingredients and cover with water. Simmer, covered, for several hours or overnight at back of stove. Line a large colander with muslin and strain stock. Take pieces of meat and pack them in Mason jars or freezer containers; cover with clear stock. Freeze remaining clear stock for gravies, stews, and sauces. This stock makes wonderful onion soup.

HINTS: Just as you should put up all your soup vegetables and purées in the summer, you should make all your long-cooking soup stocks in the late fall and winter. Late fall is usually the best time to get good buys on chicken and rabbit that farmers cull from their flocks. It is also a good time to go to your local slaughter-houses for good buys on soup bones. Many times, as soon as cool weather arrives, slaughterhouses are inundated with farmers' beef carcasses for processing. Many farmers do not want their soup bones, so if you put your name in early, you could be the beneficiary of a good supply of beef bones, possibly for free. These and the bones you saved from the summer can simmer happily on the woodstove all day or all night to be packaged and used year round for delicious soups and sauces. The meat from the fowl or older rabbit is even tastier than its younger version and makes wonderful soups, salads, and casseroles all year long. With meat, stocks, and vegetables all prepared at the proper times to save money on both food and energy, you can serve good meals that are not costly. Cooks without wood or coal heaters should make use of their Crock-Pots for the same purposes.

COOK'S NOTES:

Rich Chicken Stock

ABOUT 3 QUARTS

I like to save 2 or 3 chicken carcasses to make this soup, or better still, I simmer a large fowl until tender, to have stock for soups and nice chunks of chicken for salads or casseroles. Deliver me from the kind of watery chicken soup that tastes as if the chicken was barely waved over the pot.

Put water in a blender or food processor and add vegetables, cut into chunks, with salt and pepper and parsley. Blend until vegetables are puréed. Put mixture into a large, heavy kettle with chicken and water to cover. (If you do not have a blender or processor, just chop vegetables into chunks and toss them in kettle. They will be discarded later anyway, but blender method of preparing them gives broth a nice rich golden color.) Simmer everything in kettle until fowl is tender (about 3 hours). Remove fowl from kettle, take meat off bones, and return bones and skin to kettle to simmer for an additional 8–10 hours. If you haven't a wood or coal heater or a Crock-Pot, rather than use too much energy it's best to simmer on low heat for just 4 hours. Stock won't taste quite as rich, but it will certainly be better than anything you can buy commercially. Package meat and set aside in refrigerator. When stock is done, strain broth and discard chicken parts and vegetables. (Make sure you take all bits and pieces of chicken off bones before you discard them.) If you are not going to use stock right away, divide meat into freezer containers and cover with stock. Freeze any remaining stock as is or reduce it to one-fourth its volume. If you are using a Crock-Pot, set it on high and crack cover to allow it to condense. This will still cost only a few pennies. Store condensed broth in a Mason jar in refrigerator or freezer. If it has at least ½ inch of fat on top, it can safely be stored in refrigerator for up to 1 month.

1 large carrot
1 large onion
1 large stalk celery or *1 cup celery leaves*
1 tablespoon salt
½ teaspoon pepper
3 leftover chicken carcasses (save these in freezer as they come along) or *1 large fowl*
2 sprigs fresh parsley

HINTS: To reconstitute condensed stock, use 1 part stock to 3 parts water. To make gravy, use 1 part stock to 1 part water and add to pan drippings. This will make very rich-tasting gravy.

COOK'S NOTES:

Fish Stock

Homemade fish stock is neither difficult to prepare nor expensive. Most fish stores will happily part with fish heads, bones, and trimmings from filleting sole, halibut, haddock, and pollock, or you may have trimmings from freshwater fish you caught yourself, such as perch, northern or walleye pike, and pickerel. While bottled clam juice can be used, it can never replace a good fish stock.

3–4 pounds heads, bones, and trimmings from any mild-flavored fish
4 tablespoons bacon drippings
2 large cloves garlic, minced
2 large onions, chopped
1 cup chopped celery leaves and tops
3 tablespoons fresh parsley, chopped
1 large fresh cayenne pepper or ¼ teaspoon crushed red pepper flakes
1 tablespoon salt
¼ teaspoon black pepper
½ teaspoon dried marjoram leaves
½ teaspoon dried tarragon leaves
½ teaspoon dried dill seed
2 tablespoons white cooking wine
3 quarts water

Place fish parts in a large colander and rinse thoroughly. Heat bacon drippings in a large, heavy soup kettle and sauté vegetables until limp but not brown. Add fish, herbs, wine, and water. Cover and simmer for 2–3 hours. Line a large colander with muslin (not cheesecloth) and strain broth. Cool; if some broth is needed right away, refrigerate it for short-term storage. Freeze rest for later use. This stock does not keep as well in refrigerator as a meat stock does, so whatever hasn't been used within 3–4 days should be frozen.

HINTS: Use this stock to make Crabmeat Bisque (p. 48), Fish Sauce (p. 37), and fish chowders. This is also an excellent stock for poaching fish.

COOK'S NOTES:

Roux for Gravies and Cream Sauces

ABOUT ¾ CUP

Many people who love to cook still have difficulty making a smooth cream sauce or gravy. The use of a blender or food processor helps a great deal, but there is another way to get good results, and that is by using a roux. This is a mixture of fat and flour that has been blended into a smooth paste. It can be added to hot liquids as needed to thicken. Stir constantly while adding roux to liquids and give each addition time to become incorporated before adding more; otherwise, you will have too thick a sauce.

Heat butter in a heavy saucepan or skillet until melted. Stir in flour and cook until bubbly. Put mixture in a covered container, label, and store in refrigerator to be used as needed.

1 cup butter or fat
1 cup all-purpose flour

HINTS: I like to make four different mixtures: one made with butter for cream sauces and soups, and a chicken, a beef, and a pork roux made with rendered drippings for gravies. These give your gravies a more robust taste. Be sure to label them accurately.

COOK'S NOTES:

All-Purpose White Sauce

1 CUP

Medium
1 cup milk
2 tablespoons butter
2 tablespoons flour
½ teaspoon salt
Dash pepper

Thick
1 cup milk
3 tablespoons butter
3 tablespoons flour
½ teaspoon salt
Dash pepper

Blend all ingredients thoroughly in a blender or food processor and cook over boiling water until thick, stirring constantly.

HINTS: For a quick and easy cheese sauce, add 1 cup (4 ounces) your favorite grated cheese after the white sauce has thickened; continue cooking and stirring for another 1–2 minutes until the cheese has melted.

Velouté Sauce I

1½ CUPS

3 tablespoons butter
3 tablespoons flour
1 cup Rich Chicken Stock (p. 33)
⅓ cup heavy cream
½ teaspoon salt

Blend butter, flour, and stock in a blender or food processor until smooth. Cook over low heat in a heavy 1-quart saucepan stirring constantly, until thickened. Stir in cream and salt and heat, but do not boil.

HINTS: Purée leftover homemade soups for cream sauces to be used in casserole dishes. They make excellent substitutes for canned soups called for in many recipes. Package them in 12-ounce containers. Label them with the date, name of the soup, and dominating flavor, or the source of the recipe, so that you will know which kinds of food they will blend well with. Example: Velvety Tomato Cheese Soup (p. 61) makes a delicious sauce for pasta.

COOK'S NOTES:

Velouté Sauce II

Blend all ingredients except cream in a blender or food processor until very smooth. Cook over medium heat in a heavy 1-quart saucepan until hot and thick; stir in cream.

HINTS: This sauce freezes beautifully and reheats without separating.

1 cup bland vegetables, cooked (potatoes, summer squash, cauliflower, etc.)
1 cup Rich Chicken Stock (p. 33)
1 tablespoon butter
1 tablespoon flour (omit with potato)
½ teaspoon salt
½ cup light cream

Fish Sauce

ABOUT 2 CUPS

Blend all ingredients in a blender or food processor until smooth. Pour into a heavy 1-quart saucepan and cook over medium heat, stirring constantly, until thickened.

HINTS: This is a subtle fish sauce that can be used in any seafood casserole calling for a cream sauce or cream soup. It also makes a delicious sauce for any fish dish, such as Baked Fillet of Sole with Spinach (p. 112).

6 tablespoons minced clams and their broth
½ cup Rich Chicken Stock (p. 33)
½ cup milk
4 tablespoons all-purpose unbleached flour
Dash hot pepper sauce
1 tablespoon fresh parsley, chopped
2 tablespoons butter
½ teaspoon salt
Dash pepper
1 tablespoon lemon juice

COOK'S NOTES:

Creamy Horseradish Sauce

½ cup prepared horseradish
½ cup mayonnaise
1 tablespoon honey

Blend ingredients and store in refrigerator in a covered container. This is delicious served with hot or cold ham, boiled beef, or corned beef.

Hot Orange Mustard Sauce

2 tablespoons dry mustard
2 tablespoons cold water
1 cup orange marmalade
⅛ teaspoon garlic powder
Dash salt

Mix dry mustard with cold water. Let stand 5 minutes, then blend well into marmalade. Add garlic powder and salt and stir again to blend. Blender makes it very smooth. Sauce does not need to be refrigerated.

HINTS: I personally like to heat this sauce when I serve it with duck, but it may be served at room temperature or even cold. It is very good with Chinese food, especially Chinese Egg Rolls (p. 126). *Caution:* This sauce is definitely for those with adventuresome palates. All others should proceed with caution when adding the dry mustard mix; add a little, and then taste before going on.

COOK'S NOTES:

Sweet and Sour Sauce

7 CUPS

Put tomatoes and onion in a blender or food processor and blend until smooth. Pour into a heavy 3-quart saucepan. Add all other ingredients except peach preserves and simmer, uncovered, for 1 hour, until thickened. Add preserves and simmer a few minutes longer to incorporate flavors. Pour into hot sterilized jars and seal. Process for 5 minutes in a hot water bath canner or refrigerate. Sauce will keep in refrigerator for several months without spoiling.

HINTS: This sauce is very good as a glaze for Baked Spareribs with Sweet and Sour Sauce (p. 85), for Sweet and Sour Rabbit (p. 103), or for any type of poultry. It can be made from home-preserved foods you have on your shelves all year round.

2 cups canned tomatoes in purée
2 cups chopped onion
2 cups unsweetened applesauce
½ cup honey
1 cup cider vinegar
⅛ teaspoon pepper
1 teaspoon salt
½ teaspoon cinnamon
½ teaspoon allspice
1 teaspoon garlic powder
½ teaspoon hot pepper sauce
1¾ cups peach preserves or jam

COOK'S NOTES:

Toppings, Stuffings, and Seasonings

Buttered Crumb Topping

2 CUPS

Crispy buttered toppings do so much for a casserole that, whenever possible, I like to add them.

2 cups coarsely crushed crackers
    or coarse dried bread crumbs
4 tablespoons butter

Place crackers or bread crumbs in a small, heavy frying pan with butter. Cook and stir over medium heat until butter is melted and crumbs are well coated and slightly browned. Store in covered container in refrigerator or freezer.

HINTS: My recipes already include timing for the toppings, but if you are adapting your own recipe, do not add the toppings until 20–30 minutes before the total baking time is up. Add them quickly and continue baking, vented in position 2. You should add 10 minutes to the total baking time of the recipe to make up for heat lost when you removed the oven cover.

COOK'S NOTES:

Homemade Stuffing Mix

6 CUPS

Coarsely crumb bread in a blender or food processor, or cube very fine. Mix well with seasonings. Spread out on cookie sheets to dry, stirring occasionally. When thoroughly dry, store in a covered container in a cool, dry place. May be frozen.

HINTS: As they come along, freeze all pieces of stale toast or bread in a bag until you have enough for this dressing. One-half cup of this dry mix tossed with **2** tablespoons melted butter makes a tasty topping for many casseroles.

1½ pounds stale bread (slightly dried fresh bread may be used)
2½ tablespoons Homemade Poultry Seasoning (p. 42)
1 tablespoon salt

Homemade Stuffing for Meat and Poultry

4 CUPS WITH SAUSAGE, 3 CUPS WITHOUT

Sauté sausage with onion, celery, and parsley until sausage is well cooked. (If you omit sausage, sauté vegetables in ½ cup pork drippings or butter.) Add to stuffing mix with stock and salt. Add more stock or hot water, if necessary, to make dressing hold together. Be careful not to add too much unless you like a very wet dressing. Adjust salt to taste.

HINTS: Try this dressing with **Baked Stuffed Pork Steak (p. 79).**

1 pound country-style bulk sausage (optional)
1 cup diced onion
1 cup diced celery
2 tablespoons fresh parsley, diced fine or 1 tablespoon dried parsley
5 cups Homemade Stuffing Mix (preceding recipe)
At least ½ cup Rich Chicken Stock (p. 33)
Salt to taste

COOK'S NOTES:

Homemade Poultry Seasoning

ABOUT ⅔ CUP

4 tablespoons dried sage
4 tablespoons dried rosemary
4 teaspoons dried thyme
4 teaspoons dried oregano
2 teaspoons dried summer savory
2 teaspoons powdered ginger
1 teaspoon pepper
2 teaspoons salt

Place all ingredients in a blender and pulverize. Store in a cool place in a small airtight container. Winter savory may be substituted for summer savory, and mortar and pestle may be used if you haven't a blender.

HINTS: Do not run the blender too long. It takes only a few seconds to pulverize this mixture. Anything beyond that heats the herbs and destroys some of their flavor.

"Fines Herbes"

Parsley
Chives
Tarragon
Chervil

Commercially prepared "Fines Herbes" (finely chopped herbs) are very expensive, but you can prepare them right at home for nothing if you grow your own herbs. They are simply made up of equal parts of the following herbs, dried or fresh:

HINTS: When using fresh herbs, make sure to use 3 times the amount of dried herbs called for in a recipe. Because this preparation of herbs is so expensive in the market, you might want to make up pretty jars of the dried variety to use as gifts.

COOK'S NOTES:

Pastry

The Secret of Making Good Piecrust

The secret to a good pie is often in the crust. No matter how delicious the filling, if the crust is tough or soggy you cannot enjoy it. To prevent this from happening, try the following tips:

Handle your piecrust mix as little as possible. The more you handle the dough, the less flaky it will be.

Use only enough water to hold the crust together. Too much water will make a crust tough. The water should always be ice cold.

To prevent the bottom crust from becoming soggy, beat lightly with a fork a mixture of 1 tablespoon egg white and 1 tablespoon cold water. Brush it lightly all over the unbaked bottom crust. This will set as your crust begins to bake, sealing the bottom crust and preventing sogginess.

To have a picture-pretty flaky top crust, brush the top of the crust with softened butter. Over the butter sprinkle flour very lightly. Drizzle a couple of teaspoons of milk or cream over this and blend all ingredients together with a pastry brush so they form a light pastelike glaze. This will brown beautifully and be very flaky.

When making fruit pies, add a sprinkling of granulated sugar to the top crust.

To brown the edges of single-crust pies, brush lightly with cream or with a lightly beaten egg.

Homemade Biscuit Mix

10 CUPS

9 cups all-purpose unbleached
    flour
1 tablespoon salt
6 tablespoons double-acting
    baking powder
2 cups lard

Sift dry ingredients together several times. Cut in lard with a pastry blender or electric mixer until it resembles coarse meal. This will keep indefinitely stored in a closed container in refrigerator, or it may be frozen.

HINTS: **This cookbook contains several recipes using this mix. You can use it, however, in any recipe calling for a commercial biscuit mix.**

Quick and Easy Piecrust

1 SINGLE-CRUST PIE

1 tablespoon soft butter
2–2½ tablespoons ice water
1 cup Homemade Biscuit Mix
    (preceding recipe)

Preheat cast-iron oven to a baking temperature of 375°F. Blend butter and ice water with biscuit mix, using just enough water to hold mix together. Press mixture into a ball. Place dough on a floured surface and cover with an inverted mixing bowl. Let stand about 15 minutes to give water time to soften mix. Roll out very thin and fit into an 8–9-inch Pyrex pie plate. Trim and flute edge. Prick sides and bottom if crust is to be baked unfilled. Brush edges with cream or beaten egg. Bake, vented in position 2, for 20 minutes.

HINTS: **See piecrust tips, page 43.**

COOK'S NOTES:

Rich Piecrust

Preheat cast-iron oven to a baking temperature of 375°F. Stir flour and salt together. Add lard and butter and cut in with a pastry cutter or electric mixer. (I find that a mixer works very well, but be careful not to mix too long or mixture will become warm and make a tough crust.) Sprinkle in ice water with a fork, using just enough to hold pastry together. Let set 5 minutes to soften dough. Roll out on a floured board and fit into a 9-inch Pyrex pie plate. To bake single crusts for pies that do not require cooking, prick sides and bottom and bake, vented in position 2, for 20 minutes.

2 cups all-purpose unbleached flour
¼ teaspoon salt
½ cup lard
3 tablespoons butter
4–5 tablespoons ice water

HINTS: **See piecrust tips, page 43.**

Graham Cracker Crust

ONE 9-INCH CRUST

Crumb graham crackers in a blender or food processor until very fine. Pour into a 9-inch Pyrex pie plate sprayed with vegetable oil. Mix in sugar and cinnamon and stir in melted butter with a fork. Press mixture onto bottom and sides of pie plate. Chill.

1¼ cups graham crackers (20–22 crackers)
4 tablespoons sugar
¼ teaspoon cinnamon
½ cup melted butter

HINTS: **Use with Cheesecake (p. 152) or your favorite pudding.**

COOK'S NOTES:

Cream Puffs

10 MEDIUM CREAM PUFFS

I knew that if I could bake cream puffs in a cast-iron oven, I could bake anything. But I have to admit that it was the only recipe I had to bake over and over again before I achieved success. There are three secrets to this success: paper towels, the size of the cream puffs, and the cook's ability to bake them without peeking.

⅓ cup hot water
3 tablespoons butter
¼ teaspoon salt
¼ teaspoon carob powder (for added color)
⅓ cup flour
1 extra-large egg

Preheat cast-iron oven to a baking temperature of 375–400°F. Heat water, butter, and salt in a heavy 1-quart saucepan until butter is melted. Remove pan from heat and stir in flour all at once (a wooden spoon works best). Return saucepan to heat and cook, stirring constantly, for about 2 minutes, until mixture leaves sides of pan and forms a smooth paste that does not separate easily. Remove from heat; add egg and beat rapidly until egg is incorporated and mixture is smooth and glossy. Drop by tablespoonfuls in a shallow Pyrex baking dish that has been *lightly* sprayed with vegetable oil. Leave space between each puff. Cover with paper towels (see Paper Towel Method, p. 22) and bake, vented in position 2, for 40 minutes. *Do not peek!* Remove oven cover and paper towel arrangement. Pierce each puff with a sharp knife or skewer. Immediately replace oven cover, move venting to position 3, and *remove oven from source of heat*. Allow puffs to cool in oven 25 minutes, remove from oven, and finish cooling on a cake rack.

HINTS: This recipe will make about 24 miniature puffs that can be stuffed with your choice of fillings to be served as hors d'oeuvres.

COOK'S NOTES:

Soups

Crabmeat Bisque

6½ CUPS

1 pound king crab legs (about
    1½ cups crabmeat)
2 ounces finely diced side pork
    (unsalted bacon) or salt pork
2 tablespoons butter
½ cup sliced scallions (be sure to
    include some of the green)
¼ cup diced green pepper
¼ cup diced sweet red pepper or
    1 finely diced pimiento
½ cup diced celery
½ cup diced carrot
½ cup fresh or frozen
    mushrooms, sliced
2 tablespoons fresh parsley,
    chopped fine
1 cup stock from cooking crab
    shells or 1 cup Fish Stock
    (p. 34)
2 cups cold milk
2 tablespoons tomato paste
1½ teaspoons salt (omit ½
    teaspoon with salt pork)
¼ teaspoon pepper
⅛ teaspoon hot pepper sauce
4 tablespoons all-purpose flour
1 cup light cream
3 tablespoons cooking sherry
Butter
Paprika
Finely chopped chives

Cook crab legs if fresh or defrost if frozen and carefully remove meat. Cut into bite-sized pieces and set aside. Crush shells with a hammer and place in a saucepan; cover with cold water and bring to a boil. Simmer, covered, for at least 1 hour. Strain and reserve 1 cup stock for Bisque. Freeze remaining stock for other fish soups or casseroles. While crab shells are cooking, cook pork in a heavy 2–3-quart saucepan until fat is rendered from it, being careful not to brown fat. Remove pork from pan and discard. Add butter and vegetables, and sauté vegetables until they are limp but not brown. Add stock, cover and simmer until vegetables are tender. Blend 1 cup of the milk, tomato paste, and seasonings with flour and add to pot. Bring to a boil and simmer uncovered for 5 minutes, stirring constantly. Add crabmeat and remaining milk with cream and sherry and reheat till piping hot; do not boil. Pour into heated tureen. Float a large pat of butter on top and sprinkle lightly with paprika and chives. This makes 4 generous servings and can easily be doubled.

HINTS: This is really a party type of chowder because it is more expensive to make than everyday soups or chowders, but it's economical to serve when entertaining because it needs only the addition of crusty French bread or hard rolls, a light wine such as a chilled Chablis or French Colombard, and a dessert to round out the meal. It's so pretty with its bits of red, green, and pink that it should be served right at the table in your best soup tureen. If you are ever lucky enough to have any left over, it can be puréed and frozen to be used later as a sauce for casseroles such as Shrimp Cauliflower Supreme (p. 107), Tuna Noodle Casserole (p. 113), and Seafood Casserole (p. 108).

COOK'S NOTES:

Tuna Chowder

Sauté onion, celery, and parsley in drippings until tender. Add potatoes, peas, seasonings, and water. Cover and simmer for 10–12 minutes until potatoes are tender. Add tuna, mushrooms, and milk. Reheat to just below boiling.

HINTS: One and one-half cups of this very good, economical chowder contain approximately 23 grams of protein, equal to 3½ ounces of meat, yet it costs only about $.45 per serving. Puréed, it makes a very good sauce for Tuna Noodle Casserole (p. 113), Shrimp Cauliflower Supreme (p. 107), or any seafood casserole.

1 large onion, diced
2 large stalks celery, diced
2 tablespoons fresh parsley, diced fine or 1 tablespoon dried parsley
3 tablespoons bacon drippings or butter
1½ cups diced potatoes
2 cups frozen peas
1 tablespoon salt
½ teaspoon black pepper
2 dashes cayenne pepper
¼ teaspoon mace
1½ cups water
12 ounces drained tuna fish
½ cup cooked mushrooms, drained (optional)
4 cups milk

COOK'S NOTES:

Cream of Chicken Soup

7 CUPS

1 large onion, diced
1 large carrot, diced
1 large stalk celery, diced
2 tablespoons chicken fat or
    butter
2 cups Rich Chicken Stock (p. 33)
1 teaspoon salt
¼ teaspoon pepper
4 tablespoons all-purpose flour
2 cups cooked chicken, diced
2 cups light cream or milk
Fresh parsley for garnish

Sauté vegetables in fat in a heavy 4-quart saucepan until limp but not brown. Add stock and salt and pepper. Simmer, covered, until vegetables are very tender. Purée vegetables in a blender or food processor with flour and some stock until very smooth. Return mixture to rest of stock in pan. Add chicken and bring to a boil, then simmer for 5 minutes, stirring constantly. Add cream or milk and heat just until soup is hot. Serve topped with finely diced parsley.

HINTS: This soup makes an excellent sauce for casseroles that call for cream of chicken soup. Puréed in the blender or food processor and heated with pan drippings from chicken, it becomes a very good gravy.

Chicken Noodle Soup

SERVES 6.

1 tablespoon chicken fat or butter
1 large onion, diced
1 large stalk celery, diced
1 tablespoon fresh parsley,
    chopped
1 quart Rich Chicken Stock
    (p. 33)
1 cup uncooked fine egg noodles
1 cup cooked chicken, diced
Salt and pepper to taste

Sauté onion, celery, and parsley in chicken fat until they are limp but not brown. Add stock, noodles, chicken, and salt and pepper to taste; simmer, covered, until noodles are tender, about 12–15 minutes.

COOK'S NOTES:

Hamburg Vegetable Soup

Whenever friends are around the kitchen while I am making this vegetable soup, they become quite agitated when I reach for my jar of cinnamon, thinking that I'm about to add the wrong ingredient. When I assure them that I know what I'm doing, that it's very good, and that the soup won't taste spicy, my friends remain skeptical until it's done. This soup is hearty and full flavored and has long been a favorite of our family.

Sauté beef and onions in drippings until beef has lost its red color. Add stock, seasonings, and, if necessary, just enough water to cover meat. Bring to a boil and simmer, covered 20 minutes. Add vegetables and additional water, cover and simmer until vegetables are just tender. Adjust seasonings.

HINTS: The broth may be thickened with flour and water or a Roux (p. 35) and served as a good, quick beef stew. The seasonings are right for a thick soup or stew. If more water is used to make a thinner soup, be sure to increase the seasonings proportionately.

1½ pounds ground chuck
1 cup diced onion
1 tablespoon pork drippings or butter
1 quart Beef Stock (p. 32)
1 tablespoon salt
½ teaspoon pepper
1 teaspoon cinnamon
2 tablespoons Worcestershire sauce
3 cups diced potato
2 cups diced carrot

COOK'S NOTES:

Cabbage Soup

ABOUT 10 CUPS

1½ pounds ground beef
1 cup diced onion
4 tablespoons butter
2 cups Beef Stock (p. 32)
1½ tablespoons salt
½ teaspoon pepper
½ cup tomato sauce
4 cups (packed) thinly sliced
   cabbage
1 cup diced carrot
1 cup diced celery
1½ cups diced potato

Sauté beef and onion in butter until beef has lost its red color. Add beef stock, salt and pepper, and tomato sauce. Cover and simmer for 1 hour. Add cabbage, carrot, and celery and enough additional beef stock or water to barely come to top of vegetables. Vegetables will add own juices as they cook, so don't add too much extra water or broth or soup will be too thin. Cover and simmer for 20 minutes. Add potatoes and more water if necessary and simmer until potatoes are done, about 12 minutes. Adjust seasonings.

HINTS: I love this soup, but I don't even *like* it the day it is made. It really needs to stand one day or even two to achieve its best flavor. Purée leftover soup and use as a sauce for Cabbage Casserole (p. 135).

Boiled Dinner Soup

There always seem to be broth and vegetables left from a boiled dinner, and this soup is the perfect answer for what to do with them. Mash or chop the vegetables until they are rather fine, but not puréed. Chop any small pieces of leftover meat into bite-sized pieces and add to the vegetable mixture. For each quart of broth and vegetables, add 2 tablespoons tomato paste. If the mixture is very thick, thin with water. Simmer, covered, for 20 minutes. For each quart of soup, add ½ cup uncooked macaroni or spaghetti or ¼ cup raw rice. Simmer, stirring often, until macaroni or rice is done, about 20 minutes. Adjust seasonings before serving.

HINTS: See recipe for Boiled Dinner, page 72.

COOK'S NOTES:

Split Pea Soup with Sausage Balls

10 CUPS

Break sausage up in a medium-sized bowl. Put remaining ingredients in a blender or food processor and blend into a paste. Mix well with sausage and shape mixture into small balls. Brown in a heavy skillet; drain drippings and reserve. Refrigerate sausage balls in a covered container until needed.

Rinse peas with cold water, then soak overnight in triple their volume of water. In morning, sauté vegetables in sausage drippings in a large, heavy Dutch oven or soup kettle. Add split peas, water they were soaked in, and salt and pepper. Bring to a boil and simmer, uncovered, for 2–3 hours, adding more water as necessary, until peas are mushy-tender. Stir often to prevent sticking. Add sausage balls and simmer 30 minutes longer. Adjust seasonings.

HINTS: This soup served with hot buttered Corn Bread (p. 150) is an unbeatably nutritious and filling meal.

Sausage Balls
1 pound country-style bulk
    sausage
1 egg
3 slices bread
½ cup diced onion

Soup
1 pound yellow split peas
3 large carrots, diced fine
2 large onions, diced fine
3 large outer stalks celery, diced
    fine
4 tablespoons reserved sausage
    drippings
1 tablespoon salt
½ teaspoon pepper

COOK'S NOTES:

Corn and Ham Chowder

7 CUPS

3 slices diced bacon
1 cup finely diced ham
1 tablespoon butter
1 large onion, diced
¼ cup diced green pepper
1 cup diced potato
1 cup Rich Chicken Stock, (p. 33)
 or water
2 teaspoons salt (reduce salt to 1
 teaspoon if ham is very salty)
¼ teaspoon pepper
2½ cups milk
1 cup cream-style corn
1 cup fresh or frozen whole
 kernel corn, cooked
3 tablespoons fresh parsley,
 chopped fine, for garnish

In a heavy 4-quart Dutch oven, sauté diced bacon until crispy. Remove bacon bits and reserve. Sauté ham in 2 tablespoons bacon drippings for 3 minutes. Add butter, onion, and green pepper and sauté 1 minute more. Add potato, chicken stock, and salt and pepper. Cover and simmer until potato is tender, about 10 minutes. Add milk and corn, adjust seasonings, and reheat until piping hot. Serve sprinkled with reserved bacon bits and chopped parsley.

HINTS: Leftover soup can be puréed and used as a cream sauce with vegetables or in the following dishes: Baked Stuffed Onions (p. 134), Chicken Stack-up Dinner (p. 89), Chicken Spaghetti Bake (p. 91), Scalloped Potatoes with Ham (p. 86), and Tuna Noodle Casserole (p. 113). You can add cheese for an especially flavorful cheese sauce that can be used in many ways.

COOK'S NOTES:

American-Style Minestrone

10 CUPS

Brown ham in drippings, add onion, celery, carrots, red or green pepper, and garlic and cook until vegetables are limp but not brown. Add tomatoes and seasonings; cover and simmer for 15 minutes. Add vegetable juices and potatoes; cook, covered, 10 minutes longer. Add macaroni and more water if necessary; cover and cook an additional 10 minutes. Add zucchini and kidney beans and cook another 8 minutes. Adjust seasonings and serve with side dishes of Parmesan cheese to be added according to individual taste.

HINTS: This soup is much better if made a day ahead.

HINTS: Remember that soups and stews improve with age, so make them up when you have extra time or are in the mood for cooking. Refrigerate them for a day or two, to be served as a quick, nourishing meal on a busy day, or even a day you choose to take free for yourself. It will be much more relaxing if you know that you will be able to serve a good meal with little effort on your part.

4 ounces diced smoked ham with a little fat left on it
3 tablespoons bacon drippings
1 large onion, diced
2 large stalks celery, diced
½ cup diced carrot
1 large sweet red or green pepper, diced
1 clove garlic, minced fine
1½ cups canned tomatoes in purée
2 teaspoons salt
½ teaspoon pepper
1½ teaspoons dried basil
2 quarts vegetable juices (see HINTS p. 133) or Rich Chicken Stock (p. 33)
3 large potatoes, diced
1½ cups uncooked elbow macaroni
4 small zucchini, sliced thin
½ cup kidney beans, cooked and drained
1 cup grated Parmesan cheese

COOK'S NOTES:

Lentil Soup with Sausage

SERVES 6–8 GENEROUSLY.

1 pound country-style bulk
   sausage
3 large carrots, diced
2 large onions, diced
3 large stalks celery, diced
1 tablespoon salt
½ teaspoon pepper
1 pound dried lentils, rinsed well
   in cold water
2 quarts cold water

Sauté sausage in a large Dutch oven or heavy soup kettle until it is very well browned, but not hard and crisp. Drain sausage, return 4 tablespoons drippings to kettle, and sauté vegetables until limp but not brown. Return sausage to kettle with salt, pepper, and lentils. Add water and bring to a boil. Simmer, uncovered, for about 1 hour or until tender. Do not overcook. Stir often to prevent sticking and add water when necessary. Adjust seasonings before serving.

HINTS: A wineglass of Madeira stirred in at the very last is a tasty addition to this soup.

COOK'S NOTES:

Meatless Soups

Cream of Fresh Asparagus Soup

SERVES 4.

4 cups fresh asparagus
1 small onion
2 tablespoons butter
2 cups Rich Chicken Stock (p. 33)
1 teaspoon salt
⅛ teaspoon pepper
2 cups rich milk or 1 cup milk
 and 1 cup half-and-half

Cut asparagus into 1-inch pieces (do not use woody parts of stalk). Sauté onion in butter until limp but not brown; add asparagus, chicken stock, and seasonings and simmer, covered, until very tender, about 15 minutes. Pour this mixture into a blender or food processor and purée until smooth. Return puréed vegetables to pan, add milk, adjust seasonings, and reheat.

HINTS: Remove about ½ cup of the asparagus tips and set aside when they are cooked to just tender-crisp. Add to soup as you add milk. This makes a prettier soup, as well as giving some contrast in textures.

Broccoli Cheese Soup

SERVES 4–6.

3 cups fresh or frozen broccoli
½ teaspoon dried marjoram
 (optional)
1 cup Rich Chicken Stock (p. 33)
1 cup grated cheddar cheese
 (4 oz.)
2 tablespoons butter
2 cups rich milk or 1 cup milk
 and 1 cup half-and-half
Salt and pepper to taste

In a heavy 2-quart saucepan, simmer broccoli, marjoram, and chicken stock until broccoli is very tender. Put cubed cheese into a blender or food processor, add broccoli mixture, a little at a time, and purée until very smooth. Return to pan and add remaining ingredients. Reheat to simmer, stirring to melt cheese. Remove from heat as soon as cheese is completely melted. Adjust seasoning.

HINTS: When broccoli buds are just tender-crisp, remove a few small pieces and set aside to add at the last minute for garnish. This soup is equally good made with cauliflower or asparagus. Omit marjoram for these vegetables and add an appropriate herb, such as tarragon or dill.

COOK'S NOTES:

Cream of Celery Soup

5 CUPS

Sauté onion in butter in a heavy 2-quart saucepan until limp but not brown. Add celery, chicken stock, seasonings, and parsley. Simmer, covered, for 8 minutes. Remove 1 cup celery slices with a slotted spoon and set aside. Simmer remaining celery mixture for about 20 minutes until celery is mushy-tender. Pour into a blender or food processor and purée until smooth. Return to saucepan; add reserved celery and cream or milk. Reheat until just piping hot.

1 small onion, diced
2 tablespoons butter
4 cups thin-sliced celery
2 cups Rich Chicken Stock (p. 33)
1½ teaspoons salt
⅛ teaspoon black pepper
Dash cayenne pepper
1 teaspoon fresh parsley, chopped
1 cup light cream or milk

HINTS: To use this soup as a substitute for the commercially prepared cream of celery soup called for in many recipes, thicken it with 1–2 tablespoons flour per cup of soup. Make up some of the soup base with extra celery from the garden, omit cream, and freeze for winter use.

COOK'S NOTES:

Cream of Mushroom Soup

4 tablespoons chopped onion

4 cups fresh or frozen
    mushrooms, sliced

4 tablespoons butter

2 dashes cayenne pepper

1 cup Rich Chicken Stock (p. 33)

1 teaspoon salt

⅛ teaspoon black pepper

⅛ teaspoon garlic powder

4 cups milk

2 tablespoons flour

1 cup light cream,
    half-and-half, or additional
    milk

4 tablespoons cooking sherry
    (optional, but it makes the
    soup)

Sauté onion and mushroom in butter with cayenne pepper until tender. Remove from heat and set aside 1 cup mushroom slices with a slotted spoon. Put remaining slices in a blender or food processor with chicken stock, seasonings, milk, and flour. (You will have to do this a little at a time until everything is puréed.) Blend until very smooth. Return to pan and reheat to simmer. Heat at least 3 minutes to cook flour, stirring constantly. Add cream, optional sherry, and reserved mushrooms and reheat.

HINTS: **This is absolutely the best mushroom soup I have ever eaten! It makes a wonderful sauce for any casserole that calls for a cream sauce or canned mushroom soup.**

COOK'S NOTES:

Creamed Sugar Snap Pea Soup with Tarragon

6 CUPS

Remove stem ends from sugar snap peas. Rinse and drain. Cut onion or leeks into small pieces. (Rinse leeks carefully to remove hidden soil.) In a heavy 2-quart saucepan, sauté onion or leeks in butter until limp. Add peas, chicken stock, and seasonings. Cover and cook over low heat until vegetables are mushy-tender, about 25 minutes. Pour pea mixture into a blender or food processor a little at a time. Purée until mixture is liquified. Strain through a sieve or food mill to remove tough fibers. Add cream and chill. This is also good hot. Heat just until it is piping hot; *do not boil.*

1 pound fresh or frozen sugar snap peas
1 large sweet onion or 2 leeks
2 tablespoons butter
2½ cups Rich Chicken Stock (p. 33)
1 teaspoon dried tarragon leaves
½ teaspoon salt
⅛ teaspoon pepper
1 cup light cream

HINTS: This is one of the best *cold* soups I have ever eaten. Freeze purée of sugar snap peas in the summer when the vegetables are prolific, and you'll have delicious winter soups.

Velvety Tomato Cheese Soup

5 CUPS

Sauté onion in butter until tender, add tomatoes and salt and pepper. Cover and simmer for 20 minutes. For a chunky cheese soup, chop up cheese and add it to soup, stirring until melted. To get a velvety smooth cheese soup, add cheese to a blender or food processor with tomato mixture, a little at a time, and reheat for just 1 minute.

1 large onion, diced
2 tablespoons butter
1 quart canned tomatoes
Salt and pepper to taste
1½ cups American-type processed cheese (6 oz.)

HINTS: Cheddar cheese may be used for this recipe, but it does not give as smooth and creamy a taste as the processed cheese. For an added treat, try this recipe in the summer with 6 large fresh tomatoes, blanched, peeled, and chopped. It has a totally different flavor that is absolutely delicious. Leftover soup makes a very good sauce for baked rice or pasta dishes.

COOK'S NOTES:

Quick Spaghetti Soup

SERVES 3–4.

Many people don't use the drippings from roast pork to make gravy, but they make a very flavorful base for this quick soup. After roasting a pork, add ½ cup cold water to the drippings in the pan and simmer, scraping up all the little bits of brown that have stuck to the pan. Put this broth in a jar and refrigerate until needed.

1 large onion, diced
2 stalks celery, diced
2 tablespoons congealed pork fat
  from top of drippings
1 cup tomato sauce
Brown part of pork drippings
2½–3 cups water
Salt and pepper to taste
⅔ cup broken pieces of spaghetti
  or elbow macaroni

Sauté onion and celery in pork fat until tender; add tomato sauce, brown drippings, water, and salt and pepper. (Let your tongue be your guide for seasoning, because the meat drippings will probably contain a lot of flavor already.) Bring to a boil and simmer for 5 minutes. Add pasta and simmer, covered, until it is tender, about 15 minutes at most.

HINTS: **Small pieces of diced roast pork would be a welcome addition to this soup.**

COOK'S NOTES:

Main Dishes

Prime Rib Roast of Beef

SERVES 14–16.

Occasionally you may like to serve a large roast for a company dinner; these larger roasts can be cooked the energy-saving way by making use of an agateware roaster.

1 large piece suet
6–8-pound prime rib roast of beef
Salt and pepper to taste

Preheat *stovetop* to 450–500°F. Render half the suet in bottom of roaster. Brown roast well on all sides. Remove from roaster and put a meat rack in roaster; place roast on rack and insert meat thermometer. Cut remaining piece of suet into small pieces and dot top of roast with them. Salt and pepper lightly. Put cover on roaster with vent holes closed. Put heavy metal trivet on stovetop (it should not stand more than half an inch off stovetop) and place roaster on top of trivet. Put stovetop thermometer on roaster cover and roast, unvented, until thermometer registers a temperature that corresponds with a baking temperature of 325°F on *your* roaster chart. Open all vent holes and roast to desired doneness according to meat charts available in most cookbooks, using stove dampers to keep temperature from rising too high. (I find that if I maintain a stovetop temperature of 450–500°F on my stove, I can roast a 7-pound prime rib to medium rare in about 3 hours. This is exactly what the meat-roasting charts recommend.) Let stand 15–20 minutes to set juices. Add water and seasonings to pan drippings to make au jus gravy.

HINTS: To make carving and serving this cut of meat easier, cut meat away from rib bones before bringing roast to table.

COOK'S NOTES:

Roast Beef with Yorkshire Pudding

SERVES 6–8.

Years ago, Yorkshire pudding was baked in large batches under the roast to catch the drippings. Today, it can be baked in smaller amounts, as in this recipe, with the same delicious flavor. You might have to forgo pan gravy with a small roast such as this, but if you love Yorkshire pudding, it's well worth it. Removing a few tablespoons of drippings to add to the batter in another baking pan would give you both the pudding and the pan gravy, but the pudding would be far less tasty than the recipe as given here.

Preheat cast-iron oven to a baking temperature of 325°F. Render suet in a large, heavy skillet. Brown roast well on all sides. Place heavy metal trivet in bottom of cast-iron oven with 8–9-inch metal (not foil) cake tin on trivet (to serve as drippings pan). Add baking rack; place browned roast on rack and insert meat thermometer (see sketch). Sprinkle with pepper. Cover oven and roast beef, unvented, for 20 minutes. Vent in position 1 and roast at 325°F. to desired doneness according to meat-roasting charts available in most cookbooks. Remove from oven to warm platter. While roast is setting its juices, make Yorkshire pudding.

Lift drippings pan to top of baking rack. If roast was especially fatty, skim some fat from drippings, but be sure to leave at least 4 tablespoons. Cover cast-iron oven tightly while preparing batter, in order to recover heat. If possible, raise stove temperature to start pudding; this is not absolutely necessary as long as drippings pan is very hot. Place all pudding ingredients in a blender or food processor and blend until smooth. After cast-iron oven has had about 10 minutes to recover heat, pour batter directly into drippings pan. Vent in position 2 and bake for 20–25 minutes. Serve hot with roast.

HINTS: If you are lucky enough to have some beef gravy salted away in the freezer from a previous roast, you can have your pudding and top it with gravy too.

COOK'S NOTES:

Placement of roasting pans and racks for roast beef with Yorkshire pudding.

Roast Beef
1 small piece suet
3½–4-pound top round or sirloin tip boneless roast of beef, well covered with fat
Freshly ground pepper to taste

Yorkshire Pudding
Pan drippings
1 egg
½ cup milk
½ cup all-purpose unbleached flour
½ teaspoon salt
¼ teaspoon pepper

Small roast (about 4 lbs.) can be done in Dutch oven. Larger ones have to be done in larger pot such

Beef in Burgundy Sauce

SERVES 4–6.

1 ½ *pounds lean boneless beef,*
   cut into 1-inch pieces
1 ½ *cups Burgundy wine*
3 *ounces diced side pork*
   (unsalted bacon)
½ *cup all-purpose flour*
At least ¼ cup butter
At least ¼ cup oil
1 *large clove garlic, minced*
1 *cup tiny whole mushrooms or*
   sliced mushrooms with stems
8–10 *small whole onions, peeled*
2 *medium carrots, cut into*
   ½-inch chunks
1 *sprig fresh parsley, chopped*
   fine
¼ *cup brandy or 1 tablespoon*
   brandy extract
2 *cups Beef Stock (p. 32)*
1 *tablespoon tomato paste*
1 *teaspoon salt*
¼ *teaspoon pepper*
1 ½ *teaspoons honey*
Roux (p. 35)

Marinate beef in wine at least 4 hours. Drain well and pat dry. Reserve wine. In a heavy 4–6-quart Dutch oven, render pork, being careful not to brown meat. Remove bits of rendered pork from pan and discard. Toss beef cubes with flour to coat. Add 2 tablespoons of the butter and 2 tablespoons of the oil to the Dutch oven with the pork drippings and brown one half of the meat at a time, removing each piece to a bowl as it is browned. Add remaining butter and oil and brown rest of beef. Set beef aside. Sauté garlic and mushrooms until just lightly browned; remove from Dutch oven. Sauté onions and carrots in same way as mushrooms, adding more butter and oil if necessary. When all vegetables are lightly browned, return meat and vegetables to pan. Add wine from marinade and remaining ingredients except roux. Cover and simmer until beef is tender, 1½–2 hours. Thicken sauce with roux, adding just a tablespoon at a time to bubbling liquid and stirring constantly until it is completely incorporated. Serve with boiled parslied new potatoes or hot buttered parslied noodles.

HINTS: As with all stews, this is much better made a day ahead and reheated at serving time. The recipe can be doubled or tripled easily for company dinners.

COOK'S NOTES:

"Best" Beef Stew

SERVES 4.

Every household has a day now and then when schedules are so conflicting that it's almost impossible to plan a dinner hour convenient to everyone. On days like this, I prefer to make a dish that can be prepared even a day in advance and reheated in single-serving portions to accommodate each person's schedule. This stew is a favorite choice. It's hearty, tasty, and even better on the second or third day. Despite its many ingredients, it's quick and easy to prepare.

Melt bacon drippings in a heavy Dutch oven and sauté beef and shallot until beef is well browned. Add remaining ingredients except vegetables and roux. Simmer, covered, until beef is tender, 1½–2 hours. Add carrots, onions, and turnip and more water if necessary. Cover and cook 15 minutes longer. Add potatoes and celery; cover and cook 10 minutes more. Add peas and cook an additional 6 minutes. Thicken with roux or a mixture of flour and water.

HINTS: Leftover roast beef and gravy may be substituted for the raw beef and part of the stock. Reduce cooking time by about one-half.

HINTS: Save diced leftover meats of all kinds for a variety of soups, stews, and casseroles. Wrap them in plastic and label and date them. Don't just throw the packages in the freezer where they can get lost; put them all together in a large can or jar so you can find whatever you want quickly when the need arises.

2 tablespoons bacon drippings
1 pound lean beef, cut into
   1-inch cubes
1 finely diced shallot
1½ cups Beef Stock (p. 32) or
   water
1½ teaspoons salt
⅛ teaspoon pepper
1 tablespoon chopped parsley
2 teaspoons Worcestershire sauce
½ teaspoon allspice
1 tablespoon tomato paste
4 tablespoons red cooking wine
1 cup carrots, cut into 1-inch
   chunks
3 medium onions, cut into 4
   wedges
⅓ cup turnip, cut into small
   pieces
4 medium potatoes, cut into
   1-inch chunks
½ cup celery, cut into ½-inch
   chunks
½ cup fresh or frozen peas
Roux (p. 35)

COOK'S NOTES:

Italian Pot Roast of Beef with Noodles

SERVES 6.

1 small piece suet
1 tablespoon butter
1 clove garlic, minced very fine
1 large onion, diced
2½–3-pound boneless bottom
　　round roast of beef
1 quart tomatoes
1 teaspoon salt
¼ teaspoon pepper
½ teaspoon dried oregano
1 teaspoon dried basil
12 ounces uncooked egg noodles

Render suet till crisp over medium heat in a heavy 4-quart Dutch oven; be careful not to get heat so high that suet smokes. Remove bits of suet that remain in pan and discard. Add butter and sauté garlic and onion until limp but not brown. Remove from Dutch oven and set aside. Brown beef on all sides. Return onion and garlic to Dutch oven with remaining ingredients except noodles. Cover and simmer for about 3 hours until meat is fork-tender. Remove Dutch oven from heat. Cook noodles according to package directions and drain. Transfer meat to a hot platter, stir noodles into sauce in Dutch oven, and let stand 5 minutes before serving.

HINTS: This dish is at its best when made with bottom round roast, but it also makes a very tasty way of preparing beef spareribs.

Cheeseburger Pie

SERVES 6.

1 pound very lean ground
　　chuck
¼ cup milk
½ cup catsup
½ cup dry bread crumbs
½ cup diced onion
1 teaspoon dried sweet basil
½ teaspoon salt
⅛ teaspoon pepper
1 8-inch pie crust, unbaked
　　(p. 44)
1 cup shredded cheddar cheese

Preheat cast-iron oven to a baking temperature of 375°F. Mix all ingredients except crust and cheese. Fill piecrust with mixture and bake, vented in position 1, for 45 minutes. Add cheese and bake, vented in position 1, an additional 10 minutes.

HINTS: I like to add ½ teaspoon dried basil to the dry ingredients when I make the piecrust for this pie.

A Reminder: Even if a recipe calls for a baking temperature of 375°F, you can bake it at lower temperatures, in most instances, just by baking it longer.

COOK'S NOTES:

Spicy Beef and Noodles

When you think of meat in combination with applesauce or apple cider, you seldom think of beef, but as you will see in this one-dish meal, it makes a tantalizing combination of flavors.

Coat beef cubes with flour and brown in hot oil in a heavy 4-quart Dutch oven. Add remaining ingredients except noodles; bring to a boil, cover and simmer until beef is very tender, but not falling apart, about 1½–2 hours. Add noodles to Dutch oven, simmer, stirring constantly, for about 7 minutes, until noodles are tender.

HINTS: Leftover roast beef can be used for this dish; reduce cooking time by about one-half.

1½ pounds lean beef, cut into
   1-inch cubes
¼ cup all-purpose flour
4 tablespoons cooking oil
2½ cups apple cider
2 cups Beef Stock (p. 32)
1 large onion, diced
½ teaspoon allspice
½ teaspoon cinnamon
2 teaspoons salt
¼ teaspoon pepper
2 tablespoons brown sugar
2 tablespoons Worcestershire
   sauce
8 ounces uncooked egg noodles

COOK'S NOTES:

Swiss Steak

I learned to make this Swiss steak some 30 years ago, and though I have tried other recipes since, it remains my favorite way of preparing this tasty dish.

½ cup all-purpose flour
1½ teaspoons salt
½ teaspoon pepper
1½-pound round steak, cut 1½ inches thick
3 tablespoons bacon drippings
1 small onion, diced
1½ cups stewed tomatoes or tomato juice

Mix flour, salt, and pepper; spread half the mixture on a cutting board or clean surface. Place steak on board and sprinkle with part of the remaining flour. Pound meat with a meat mallet or edge of a heavy saucer, adding more flour, until all the flour has been taken up; turn occasionally so that both sides will be equally floured. Heat bacon drippings in a large, heavy cast-iron skillet; sauté steak on both sides until nicely browned. Add onion and tomatoes, cover tightly and simmer until tender, about 1½ hours. Serve with hot mashed potatoes, using sauce as pan gravy.

HINTS: I prefer using a heavy saucer to a meat mallet; it seems to do a much better job of incorporating the flour into the meat without tearing it up. This steak freezes well and can be reheated from the frozen state in about 30 minutes in a heavy covered skillet.

COOK'S NOTES:

Meat Loaf

SERVES 6–8.

Preheat cast-iron oven to a baking temperature of 325°F. Place ground beef in a large bowl. Purée remaining ingredients in a blender or food processor; pour over meat in bowl and mix thoroughly. Turn into a 6-cup gelatin mold or tube pan sprayed with vegetable oil and bake, unvented, for 15 minutes. Vent in position 2 and continue baking 45 minutes longer. Meat loaf will pull away from sides of pan when done.

HINTS: Hot or cold, this meat loaf is attractive when turned out onto a platter and the center filled with hot mashed potatoes or your favorite vegetable. Cold, it slices nicely and makes an especially tasty sandwich.

2 pounds ground beef
2 eggs
1 large onion
3 slices bread
½ cup milk
3 tablespoons prepared mustard
2 tablespoons catsup
2 tablespoons Worcestershire sauce
1 teaspoon salt
¼ teaspoon pepper

Stuffed Meat Loaf

SERVES 6.

Preheat cast-iron oven to a baking temperature of 350°F. Combine all ingredients except potatoes and cheese. Mix potatoes with cheese. Divide meat mixture in half. Pat first half into an 8½- by 2-inch Pyrex baking dish sprayed with vegetable oil. Spread mashed potatoes over meat mixture and top with remaining meat mixture. Bake, vented in position 1, for 50–60 minutes.

HINTS: This meat loaf is very good served with a richly flavored tomato sauce.

2 beaten eggs
½ cup milk
2 slices bread, crumbed
½ cup diced onion
1½ teaspoons salt
½ teaspoon ground sage
⅛ teaspoon pepper
1½ pounds lean ground beef
2 cups mashed potatoes
4 ounces (1 cup) shredded cheddar cheese

COOK'S NOTES:

Boiled Dinner

SERVES 6.

3 pounds lean beef, beef
  spareribs, corned beef, or ham
1 tablespoon salt (omit with
  corned beef or ham)
1 teaspoon pepper
6 large onions
6 slices turnip
1 large cabbage, cut into 6
  wedges
9 large carrots, cut in half
2 cups whole green and yellow
  beans, in season
6 large potatoes, cut in half

Place meat in a large, heavy soup kettle or Dutch oven. Cover with cold water and add salt and pepper. Bring to a boil and simmer, covered, for 3 hours, until fork-tender. Remove meat from broth and put all vegetables except potatoes in pot. Simmer, covered, for 15 minutes. Add potatoes and put meat back on top of vegetables. Broth should cover vegetables but need not cover meat, since you need only keep meat hot while vegetables are cooking. Add water if necessary. Cover and cook until vegetables are tender. Slice meat and place in center of large platter; surround with vegetables and serve accompanied by a bowl of broth.

HINTS: A good sauce to serve with this meat is Creamy Horse-radish Sauce (p. 38). Leftover boiled dinner makes a tasty base for a hearty vegetable soup (see recipe for Boiled Dinner Soup, p. 52).

COOK'S NOTES:

All-In-One Hamburg Dinner

SERVES 4.

Preheat cast-iron oven to a baking temperature of 375°F. Mix onion and seasoning with ground beef and pat into a 2-quart casserole dish sprayed with vegetable oil. Top with green beans. Mix tomato sauce with brown sugar and pour over beans. Bake, unvented, for 30 minutes. Vent in position 2 and bake 10 minutes longer. Working quickly, top with hot mashed potatoes and bake in position 2 for an additional 30 minutes.

1 medium onion, diced
½ teaspoon salt
¼ teaspoon pepper
1 pound ground beef
2 cups French style green beans, cooked and drained well
½ cup tomato sauce
1 tablespoon brown sugar
2 cups mashed potatoes (should be slightly dry)

Lazy Day Rice Casserole

SERVES 4–6.

Preheat cast-iron oven to a baking temperature of 350°F. Mix rice, onion, green pepper, corn, and ground beef thoroughly in a 2-quart Pyrex casserole dish sprayed with vegetable oil. Mix tomato juice with brown sugar and salt and pepper; pour over rice mixture and mix well. Top with bacon strips. Bake, unvented, for 1½ hours. Vent in position 2 and bake an additional 30–45 minutes, until rice in center is well done.

HINTS: This dish is wonderful made with brown rice. Add 30 minutes to the unvented baking time. The casserole can be baked slowly for about 8 hours at a temperature of 200°F. Vent the last hour. It is also an excellent Crock-Pot recipe. Brown bacon strips first and add bacon drippings to the rice mixture, top casserole with cooked bacon strips, and cook casserole on low for 8 hours.

¾ cup raw rice, rinsed with cold water
½ cup diced onion
½ cup diced green pepper
1 cup cooked whole kernel corn, drained
½ pound uncooked ground beef
4 cups tomato juice
2 tablespoons brown sugar
1 teaspoon salt
¼ teaspoon pepper
4 slices bacon, cut in half

COOK'S NOTES:

Shepherd's Pie

SERVES 4–6.

1½ pounds ground chuck
1 large onion, diced
1½ teaspoons Homemade
   Poultry Seasoning (p. 42)
½ teaspoon salt
⅛ teaspoon pepper
2 cups cooked whole kernel corn,
   drained
3 cups potatoes
Milk to taste
Butter to taste
Salt and pepper to taste

Preheat cast-iron oven to a baking temperature of 375°F. Combine ground beef, onion, 1 teaspoon of the poultry seasoning, salt, and pepper in a saucepan with just enough water to cover. Simmer, uncovered, for 20 minutes. Place mixture in a well-greased 2-quart Pyrex casserole dish. (If broth comes above level of meat mixture, take some out, and correct seasonings.) Spread corn over meat mixture. Mash potatoes with milk, butter and remaining ½ teaspoon poultry seasoning and salt and pepper. Do not add too much milk; potatoes should be on dry side. Top casserole with potatoes. Bake, unvented, for 20 minutes. Vent in position 2 and bake until potatoes start to brown on top, about 40 minutes longer.

HINTS: Peas may be substituted for the corn in this recipe.

Stir-Fried Beef and Broccoli

SERVES 4.

1-pound round steak
2 cups broccoli
2 tablespoons peanut oil
2 tablespoons butter
½ cup blanched slivered
   almonds
1 tablespoon soy sauce
Salt and pepper to taste
Dash garlic powder (optional)

Put steak in freezer until slightly firm, but not really frozen; slice in thin strips. Break broccoli florets into small pieces; slice stalk in thin diagonal slices. Heat peanut oil and butter in a large, heavy cast-iron skillet. Add steak, broccoli, almonds, and seasonings. Stir-fry until beef is browned and broccoli is cooked tender-crisp.

HINTS: Pork steaks may be substituted for beef, but be sure to cook pork until it is well done. This takes only 1–2 minutes longer.

COOK'S NOTES:

Beef and Biscuit Topsy-Turvy

SERVES 4.

Preheat cast-iron oven to a baking temperature of 375°F. In a large, heavy iron skillet, fry bacon pieces until crisp. Drain fat and reserve. Combine tomato juice, honey, and basil in a medium-sized bowl; add bacon bits and biscuit mix all at once. Stir until mix is moistened.

Sauté onion, celery, and green pepper in bacon drippings until limp but not brown; add ground beef and seasonings. Cook until beef is nicely browned but not crisp. Purée milk, mushrooms, flour, and cheese in a blender or food processor; stir into meat mixture. Place mixture in a greased 8½- by 2-inch Pyrex baking dish. Spread topping over meat with a spoon. Bake, vented in position 2, for 20 minutes. Move venting to position 3 and bake an additional 20 minutes.

HINTS: Puréed Cream of Mushroom Soup (p. 60) may be used in place of the milk, mushrooms, and flour. Use 6 tablespoons of the soup.

Topping
3 slices diced bacon
⅔ cup tomato juice
1 teaspoon honey
½ teaspoon dried basil
1½ cups Homemade Biscuit Mix (p. 44)

Filling
½ cup diced onion
¼ cup diced celery
¼ cup diced green pepper
2 tablespoons bacon drippings (from topping)
1 pound ground beef
½ teaspoon salt
¼ teaspoon pepper
½ teaspoon dried basil
¼ cup milk
2 tablespoons chopped mushrooms
1 tablespoon flour
½ cup shredded cheddar cheese

COOK'S NOTES:

Italian Meat and Potato Casserole

SERVES 4–6.

1 pound ground beef
1 clove garlic, minced fine
1 tablespoon bacon fat
4 large fresh basil leaves,
    chopped fine or 1 teaspoon
    dried basil
1½ teaspoons fresh sage,
    chopped fine or ½ teaspoon
    dried sage
1 crushed bay leaf
2 teaspoons salt
¼ teaspoon pepper
1 teaspoon paprika
2½ cups canned tomatoes
¼ cup butter
4 medium potatoes, peeled and
    sliced thin
2 large onions, sliced thin

Preheat cast-iron oven to a baking temperature of 375°F. Brown ground beef and garlic in bacon fat in a heavy skillet. Add remaining ingredients except potatoes and onions; simmer for 10 minutes. Meanwhile, slice potatoes and onions. When meat sauce is ready, layer potatoes, onions, and sauce in a greased 2-quart casserole dish and bake, unvented, for 1 hour. Vent in position 1 and bake an additional 30–45 minutes until vegetables are done.

HINTS: New potatoes take longer to bake than old ones (winter potatoes), so be sure to allow extra time. Fifteen minutes extra is usually enough for the average casserole dish.

Corned Beef Hash

SERVES 4.

This dish is a tasty and quick meal for a busy day.

4 tablespoons bacon fat
12 ounces cooked corned beef,
    diced finely
2 large onions, diced
4 cups cooked potatoes, diced
Salt and pepper to taste

Melt fat in a large, heavy skillet. Add remaining ingredients and stir well to mix. Fry until browned on bottom. Turn with a spatula and continue to fry until all hash is well browned.

HINTS: This dish is a very good way to use up leftover corned beef and potatoes from a boiled dinner. It is especially good served with pickled beets, tossed salad, and homemade bread.

COOK'S NOTES:

Easy Pepper Steak

SERVES 6.

Steak is easier to slice in thin strips if it is partially frozen, so place it in the freezer about an hour before you are ready to prepare this dish.

Slice steak in thin strips. Mix flour, salt, and pepper in a paper bag; shake steak strips in bag to coat. Heat cooking oil in a large, heavy cast-iron skillet or wok; add steak and garlic and stir-fry until steak is brown. Add beef stock, cover and simmer for 1¼ hours. Add remaining ingredients; cover and simmer 8–10 minutes longer. Correct seasonings. For a thicker sauce, slowly add 1 tablespoon cornstarch mixed with 2 teaspoons cold water to simmering sauce, stirring constantly until as thick as desired. Serve with rice or egg noodles.

HINTS: This recipe can be made with pork steaks, but be sure to cook pork until it is well done.

1½-pound round steak
¼ cup all-purpose flour
1 teaspoon salt
⅛ teaspoon pepper
¼ cup cooking oil
1 clove garlic, minced fine
2 cups Beef Stock (p. 32)
1 large tomato, blanched, peeled, and cut into wedges
1 large onion, sliced
2 green peppers, cut in strips
1 tablespoon good soy sauce or tamari
1 tablespoon brown sugar

COOK'S NOTES:

Chili

8 CUPS

1½ pounds ground beef
2 tablespoons cooking oil
1 clove garlic, minced fine
1½ cups diced onion
1½ cups diced green pepper
4 cups canned tomatoes, drained
   of most of their juice (save for
   sauce)
2 tablespoons tomato paste
2 teaspoons chili powder
⅛ teaspoon cayenne pepper
2 bay leaves
3 cups cooked kidney beans,
   drained
1 cup shredded cheddar cheese

In a heavy Dutch oven, brown beef in oil with garlic, onion, and green pepper. Add tomatoes, tomato paste, and seasonings. Heat to boiling and simmer, uncovered, for 1 hour. Add kidney beans and simmer until thick. Serve chili in heated bowls topped with 2 tablespoons shredded cheddar per serving.

HINTS: Chili is better made early in the day or the day before serving and reheated at meal time. The longer it stands, the better the flavor. This recipe is very good served in crisp taco shells, topped with shredded lettuce, grated cheese, and diced raw onion.

Sloppy Joes

SERVES 4–6.

1 pound ground beef
¼ cup cooking oil
½ cup diced onion
½ cup diced green pepper
¼ cup diced celery
1 cup tomato sauce
¼ cup thick catsup
1 tablespoon cider vinegar
1 tablespoon prepared mustard
1 tablespoon honey
1 teaspoon salt
⅛ teaspoon pepper
1½ teaspoons Worcestershire
   sauce
2 dashes hot pepper sauce

Brown beef in hot oil in a heavy skillet. Add diced vegetables and cook until they are limp but not brown. Add remaining ingredients and simmer, uncovered, until thick, stirring occasionally (about 25 minutes). Serve on hamburg rolls.

HINTS: This makes a very good sauce for pasta.

COOK'S NOTES:

Baked Stuffed Pork Steak

SERVES 4.

Preheat cast-iron oven to a baking temperature of 325°F. Sauté onion and celery in fat till tender. Add to dry stuffing mix with just enough hot chicken stock to bind. *Do not make a wet dressing.* Add salt and pepper to taste if dressing doesn't already have enough. Pound steak with a meat mallet or edge of a heavy saucer. Spread dressing on flattened steaks to within an inch of edge. Roll steaks into tight bundles, tucking ends in. Tie with strong twine. Brown steak bundles well in hot fat on all sides, then place in a round Pyrex baking dish and sprinkle with salt and pepper. Pour pan drippings over bundles and roast, unvented, for 20 minutes. Vent in position 1 and roast for 1 hour.

HINTS: These are delicious hot or cold, sliced thin. When served cold, they turn a simple buffet of salads and rolls into something special. Beef round steaks may be substituted for pork steaks. For a nice change, dice half a peeled and cored apple and add it to stuffing when you are using pork steaks. Reduce onion to ¼ cup.

½ cup diced onion
¼ cup diced celery
2 cups Homemade Stuffing Mix (p. 41)
¼–½ cup heated Rich Chicken Stock (p. 33)
Salt and pepper to taste
1½-pound pork steak, trimmed of all fat
4 tablespoons butter or pork drippings

COOK'S NOTES:

Glazed Pork Roast

SERVES 9–10.

3–4-pound boned and rolled
 pork butt
Salt and pepper to taste
Garlic powder to taste
1 cup Sweet and Sour Sauce
 (p. 39) or peach jam

Roast pork at a baking temperature of 325°F. Remove rack from cast-iron oven and heat oven on stovetop until it is hot enough to fry in. Brown pork roast well on all sides right in oven. Remove roast from oven, return rack, and place roast directly on rack. Put meat thermometer in place (see sketch, p. 23). Sprinkle with salt, pepper, and garlic powder and roast, unvented, for 20 minutes; vent in position 1 and continue roasting according to timing given in meat-roasting charts available in most cookbooks. While pork is roasting, heat sauce for glaze in a small pan on top of oven, or on stovetop if you have room. Quickly remove roast from oven 1 hour before it is done and put it in a Pyrex baking dish. (Be sure to replace cover on oven snugly to avoid temperature loss.) Baste roast with glaze and quickly return to oven, continuing to baste every 15 minutes until roast is thoroughly done. Venting should be kept in position 2 during glazing time. When roast is cooked, remove it from oven and make gravy with pan drippings.

Note: I feel it is very important to use a meat thermometer when cooking pork. Undercooked pork can be the cause of trichinosis.

HINTS: The cut of pork known as Boston Butt is reasonably economical. Boned and rolled (tied), with a glaze, it makes a nice company meal. When buying this cut of meat, look for a nice lean butt roast *with the bone still in*. Fat roasts often will be boned and rolled in order to tuck the fat inside to hide it. So ask for a lean pork butt and check it yourself *unwrapped*. Then ask the butcher to bone and roll it for you. He might charge you a few cents extra per pound, but it will be worth it. Tell him you want the bones and trimmings; by putting them in the roasting pan along with your roast, you will get extra-nice brown drippings for a rich, full-flavored gravy.

COOK'S NOTES:

Jellied Pork Loaf

ONE 3-POUND LOAF

This recipe is a favorite at butchering time, using a part of the pig that is frequently discarded. If you are not especially fond of strong garlic, you may reduce the amount called for; however, do include at least 2 cloves for good flavor.

Scrub pork hocks with a stiff brush until thoroughly cleaned. Place all ingredients in a large cast-iron Dutch oven and cover with water. Simmer, covered, until meat falls off bones. (I cook mine all night.) Strain mixture in a colander lined with cheesecloth. Return stock to pot and simmer until reduced by one-third. Remove pieces of meat and chop coarsely. Grind rinds with a coarse blade or chop them in a food processor. Mix chopped rinds and meat with a little of the fat; discard rest. Pack meat mixture into an 8½- by 4- by 2½-inch loaf pan sprayed with vegetable oil. Pour enough of the reduced broth into pan to fill it. Cool at room temperature, stirring occasionally, for 2 hours. Cover with tinfoil and refrigerate. Stir every hour until thoroughly chilled to prevent fat from rising to top. Allow loaf to stand at least 24 hours before serving. Slice thin for sandwiches or thicker for use with salads.

4 pork hocks
6 gloves garlic, minced very fine
1 very large onion, diced
½ cup diced carrot
2 tablespoons fresh parsley, chopped
¼ cup diced celery
2 teaspoons salt
¼ teaspoon black pepper
4 dashes cayenne pepper
¼ teaspoon powdered cloves

HINTS: Since you will have twice as much broth as you will need for 1 loaf, you can double your yield by adding a rabbit to the pot along with the pork hocks. This will give you enough meat for 2 loaves. If you have problems getting this loaf to jell, it's because you haven't reduced the broth enough. To correct the problem, place the entire contents of the loaf in a heavy saucepan over low heat until all the juices are warm. Strain again and reduce the broth further. This is an excellent Crock-Pot recipe.

COOK'S NOTES:

Pork Chops with Macaroni and Tomatoes

SERVES 4.

1 teaspoon salt
⅛ teaspoon pepper
Dash paprika
½ teaspoon thyme
¼ cup all-purpose flour
Four 1-inch-thick pork chops
1 tablespoon butter
2 tablespoons cooking oil
2 cups thick tomato sauce
¼ cup red cooking wine
2 tablespoons tomato paste
½ teaspoon garlic powder
1 teaspoon salt
1 tablespoon honey
½ teaspoon thyme
¼ teaspoon pepper
2 cups cooked elbow macaroni,
    drained
¼ cup grated Parmesan cheese

Preheat cast-iron oven to a baking temperature of 375°F. Mix seasonings with flour and coat pork chops. In a large, heavy skillet, brown chops quickly in hot butter and oil. Remove chops and set aside. Add remaining ingredients except macaroni and cheese to skillet. Bring sauce to a boil and simmer, uncovered, for 10 minutes. Combine cooked macaroni and grated Parmesan with sauce. Pour into a 2-quart Pyrex baking dish sprayed with vegetable oil. Arrange pork chops on top and bake, unvented, for 30 minutes. Vent in position 1 and bake an additional 30–40 minutes.

COOK'S NOTES:

Baked Shoulder Ham

SERVES 10–12.

A whole ham is usually much too large for a small family, and a fancy smoked ham is very expensive. Small, lean smoked shoulders are a very sensible alternative, and baked according to these directions they make a nice baked ham dinner. I have always felt that they have far more flavor than the larger hams.

Preheat cast-iron oven to a baking temperature of 325°F. Parboil smoked shoulder, covered with water, for 1½ hours, with rind on. Remove meat from broth and drain well. Cut off rind but do not discard. Make sure to leave a thin layer of fat on ham for flavor and for keeping meat moist while baking. Score fat with a sharp knife. Place a meat thermometer through side of ham (see sketch p. 23) into meatiest part of shoulder. Place ham directly on baking rack in cast-iron oven, with rind lying loosely on top. Roast, unvented, for 20 minutes. Vent in position 1 and roast 1 hour. Quickly remove rind and roast in position 1 for an additional hour. Ham should register done at this point; remove from oven and put cover back on tightly to recover baking temperature as quickly as possible. Place ham in a round Pyrex baking dish and pat brown sugar mixed with cloves on top of fat part of ham. Return dish to oven. Vent in position 2 and roast an additional 20 minutes to allow sugar coating to form a glaze over ham. Serve hot or cold with gravy made with brown drippings in oven.

6-pound lean smoked shoulder
½ cup brown sugar
½ teaspoon powdered cloves

HINTS: Rind should be left over the roast for part of the roasting time in order to get brown, rich-tasting drippings for a good gravy. Leftover ham can be sliced for sandwiches, diced for Corn and Ham Chowder (p. 54), Scalloped Potatoes with Ham (p. 86), and many other dishes. Don't forget to save the soup bone for pea soup.

COOK'S NOTES:

Ham Croquettes

4 tablespoons bacon fat

5 tablespoons all-purpose flour

1 medium onion, diced

1 teaspoon salt (omit if ham is
 very salty)

⅛ teaspoon pepper

3 tablespoons prepared
 horseradish

1 teaspoon prepared mustard

Dash hot pepper sauce

¾ cup unsweetened pineapple
 juice

3 cups cooked ham, ground fine

2 eggs

¼ cup milk

1 small onion, diced

2 cups dry bread crumbs

Fat for frying

Blend first 9 ingredients in a blender or food processor until smooth. Pour into a heavy 1-quart saucepan and cook until thickened, stirring constantly. Add to ham and blend well. Turn mixture into a 9-inch pie plate sprayed with vegetable oil. Pat down firmly and chill until stiff, 4–6 hours. Cut into wedges. Purée eggs, milk, and onion in blender or food processor until smooth. Pour out into a shallow bowl. Dip ham wedges in bread crumbs, then in egg mixture, and again in bread crumbs. Coat well all over. Fry in deep fat (375°F) until golden brown and crisp. Drain on paper towels.

HINTS: Leftovers may be frozen and reheated in a cast-iron oven preheated to 375°F. Bake, vented in position 1, for 40 minutes.

COOK'S NOTES:

Baked Spareribs with Sweet and Sour Sauce

SERVES 4.

Preheat cast-iron oven to a baking temperature of 350°F. Place ribs directly on baking rack in oven. Season to taste. Bake, vented in position 1, for about 1½ hours, or until fat starts to get crisp. Working quickly, remove ribs from oven to largest shallow baking dish that will fit your oven (making sure dish is well greased). Spread sauce evenly over ribs. Return to oven and bake in position 1 an additional 45 minutes.

HINTS: These ribs can be cooked directly on the charcoal grill. Reduce timing for the higher cooking temperatures. The ribs should not be brushed with sauce until the fat is crisp, or the sauce will burn before the ribs are done.

4 pounds pork spareribs, cut into pieces 2–3 inches long
Salt and pepper to taste
Garlic powder to taste
1 cup Sweet and Sour Sauce (p. 39)

Scalloped Corn with Sausage

SERVES 6.

Preheat cast-iron oven to a baking temperature of 375°F. Cook sausage until well browned. Drain fat, set sausage aside, and return 4 tablespoons of the drippings to skillet. Add onion and green pepper and sauté until tender but not brown; combine with sausage. Mix remaining ingredients except crumb topping in a 1½-quart Pyrex baking dish sprayed with vegetable oil. Add sausage-and-onion mixture and mix well. Slip into oven quickly. Vent in position 1 and bake for 40 minutes. Lift cover quickly and add crumb topping; return cover and bake, vented in position 2, an additional 20 minutes.

HINTS: Substitute 1½ cups diced ham for sausage and use pork drippings or butter instead of sausage drippings.

1 pound country-style bulk sausage
½ cup diced onion
½ cup diced green pepper
2 cups cream-style corn
2 cups cooked whole kernel corn, drained
½ teaspoon salt
2 well beaten eggs
2 cups soft bread crumbs
¾ cup Buttered Crumb Topping (p. 40)

COOK'S NOTES:

Scalloped Potatoes with Ham

SERVES 4–6.

4 large potatoes, peeled and
    sliced thin
2 large onions, sliced thin
1 cup diced ham
2½ cups Thick White Sauce
    (p. 36) or soup purée (see
    HINTS below)
4 tablespoons ham drippings,
    bacon drippings, or butter
1 teaspoon salt
¼ teaspoon pepper

Preheat cast-iron oven to a baking temperature of 375°F. Layer potatoes, onions, and ham in a 1½-quart Pyrex casserole dish sprayed with vegetable oil. Heat sauce with seasonings and pour into casserole. Make sure sauce goes well down into bottom of dish, but do not overfill; sauce should come up level with top layer of potatoes or ham, whichever you finish with. Bake, unvented, for 30 minutes. Vent in position 1 and bake 45 minutes longer. Move venting to position 2 and bake an additional 15 minutes, or until potatoes are tender. (This will depend mostly on how thin you sliced your vegetables.

HINTS: Puréed soups that make a good sauce for this casserole are Corn and Ham Chowder (p. 54), Cream of Mushroom Soup (p. 60), and Cream of Chicken Soup (p. 50).

COOK'S NOTES:

Baked Stuffed Zucchini

SERVES 4 GENEROUSLY.

Preheat cast-iron oven to a baking temperature of 375°F. Wash zucchini and cut into slices 2½ inches thick. Place with one cut side down on a rack in a large, heavy saucepan and steam for 5 minutes. Scrape seed pod out of center and place rounds standing in a well-oiled shallow cake pan, as large as will fit your cast-iron oven. Salt zucchini well and fill centers with stuffing that has been mixed with grated Parmesan. Let dressing come up over top of squash. Put remaining ingredients except cheddar into a blender or food processor and blend thoroughly to pulverize garlic and basil leaves. Pour sauce over zucchini and sprinkle shredded cheddar over top. Bake, unvented, for 10 minutes. Vent in position 1 and bake 30 minutes longer.

HINTS: While this recipe can be made with small to medium zucchini, steamed and sliced lengthwise in boats, it is a very good way to use these prolific squashes when they have grown to be oversized.

1 large zucchini
Salt to taste
2 cups Homemade Stuffing for Meat and Poultry, with sausage (p. 41)
¼ cup grated Parmesan cheese
1 cup thick tomato sauce
2 tablespoons fresh basil
1 clove garlic
¼ teaspoon salt
⅛ teaspoon pepper
1 cup shredded cheddar cheese

COOK'S NOTES:

Poultry and Rabbit

IN THE FOLLOWING RECIPES RABBIT AND CHICKEN CAN BE USED INTERCHANGEABLY.

Stir-Fried Chicken and Sugar Snap Peas

SERVES 4.

Sugar snap peas are one of the newest and (I think) most exciting vegetable varieties to be developed in recent years. They're very sweet and can be eaten pod and all. This recipe takes less than 10 minutes to prepare.

4 tablespoons butter
1 ½ cups uncooked chicken, cut into bite-sized pieces
2 cups sugar snap peas, stem ends and strings removed
Salt and pepper to taste
Garlic powder to taste

Melt butter in a large, heavy skillet; add chicken and peas, including pod. Sprinkle with salt, pepper, and garlic powder to taste and stir-fry until chicken is cooked and peas are still tender-crisp, about 8–10 minutes. *Do not overcook.* Serve with fried rice or plain boiled rice.

HINTS: Shrimp may be substituted for chicken, but should be added just in the last few minutes. Small fresh shrimp should stir-fry in 3–4 minutes. Cooked frozen shrimp should be defrosted under running cold water. (It takes just 2 minutes to defrost them this way.) Add them to the skillet in the last 1½-2 minutes of cooking time.

COOK'S NOTES:

Chicken Stack-Up Dinner

SERVES 4.

You couldn't ask for an easier or better-tasting chicken dinner than this one.

Preheat cast-iron oven to a baking temperature of 350°F. Arrange potato and onion slices in layers in a greased 8½- by 2-inch round Pyrex baking dish. Heat chicken soup purée with salt, pepper, and poultry seasoning and pour over potatoes. Place baking dish on a rack in oven. Place another round rack over dish of potatoes and arrange chicken parts on it, directly over potatoes. Sprinkle chicken very lightly with more salt and pepper. Bake, unvented, for 30 minutes. Vent in position 1 and bake 1 hour longer. Juices from chicken will go right down into sauce, making a rich-tasting gravy for potatoes.

HINTS: Other soup purées that can be used are Cream of Mushroom Soup (p. 60) and Corn and Ham Chowder (p. 54).

4 medium potatoes, peeled and sliced thin
1 medium onion, sliced thin (optional)
1½ cups Cream of Chicken Soup purée (p. 50) or Velouté Sauce I (p. 36)
1 teaspoon salt
¼ teaspoon pepper
¼ teaspoon Homemade Poultry Seasoning (p. 42)
2-pound broiler chicken, cut into quarters

COOK'S NOTES:

Honey Soy Chicken

SERVES 4–6.

2½–3-pound fryer chicken
1 medium onion
⅓ cup honey
1 tablespoon paprika
2 tablespoons melted butter
2 tablespoons good soy sauce
Salt and pepper to taste

Preheat cast-iron oven to a baking temperature of 375°F. Rinse chicken and pat dry. Tuck onion in cavity. Combine remaining ingredients and baste chicken with mixture. Quickly slip chicken into oven, directly on rack. Roast, unvented, for 30 minutes. Quickly baste again, vent in position 2, and roast for 45 minutes. Baste again and continue roasting in position 2 for 30–45 minutes. When done, drumstick should move up and down in joint freely. Remove from oven and let stand 15 minutes to set juices.

HINTS: Make sure you baste quickly, because every time you open the oven cover, it takes that much longer to recover the proper baking temperature inside the oven. It would be a good idea to keep track of the total time it took you to roast the chicken and make a note of it below for future reference.

COOK'S NOTES:

Chicken Spaghetti Bake

SERVES 4–6.

Preheat cast-iron oven to a baking temperature of 375°F. In a heavy 2-quart saucepan, cook bacon, onion, and garlic till bacon is crisp. Stir often so onion will not get too brown. Blend in flour thoroughly; add tomatoes, Velouté sauce, mushrooms, seasonings, and tomato paste. Cook, stirring constantly, until sauce is thickened and bubbly. Stir in cheddar cheese, spaghetti, and chicken. Turn into a 2-quart Pyrex casserole dish sprayed with vegetable oil. Bake, vented in position 1, for 45 minutes. Top with Parmesan cheese and bake in position 1 an additional 15 minutes.

HINTS: Soup purées that make a good sauce for this dish are Cream of Mushroom Soup (p. 60), Cream of Chicken Soup (p. 50), and Corn and Ham Chowder (p. 54).

3 slices diced bacon
½ cup chopped onion
1 clove garlic, minced fine
3 tablespoons flour
2 cups canned tomatoes
1½ cups Velouté Sauce I (p. 36)
¼ cup finely chopped mushrooms
1 teaspoon dried sweet basil
½ teaspoon salt
¼ teaspoon pepper
2 tablespoons tomato paste
1 cup shredded cheddar cheese
2 cups cooked spaghetti (break spaghetti into small pieces before cooking)
2 cups cooked chicken, cubed
¼ cup grated Parmesan cheese

COOK'S NOTES:

Ester's Chicken Verona

1 cup fine bread crumbs
⅓ cup grated Parmesan cheese
¼ cup fresh parsley, chopped
   very fine
2 teaspoons salt
¼ teaspoon pepper
⅛ teaspoon dry mustard
¾ cup butter
1 clove garlic, minced very fine
3 pounds chicken parts

Preheat cast-iron oven to a baking temperature of 375°F. Mix bread crumbs with Parmesan, parsley, salt, pepper, and mustard. Melt butter with garlic. Dip chicken parts in butter, then in crumb mixture. Arrange chicken in a single layer in a greased shallow Pyrex baking dish. Top with any remaining crumb mixture and butter. Bake, vented in position 1, for 1¼–1½ hours, until chicken is fork-tender.

Fruited Chicken

2½-pound broiler chicken
½ cup all-purpose flour
1 teaspoon salt
¼ teaspoon pepper
1 teaspoon grated lemon rind
4 tablespoons butter
4 tablespoons peanut oil
½ cup apple cider
2 tablespoons honey
1 apple, peeled, cored, and sliced
   thin
1 peach, blanched, peeled,
   seeded, and sliced thin
¼ cup raisins

Preheat cast-iron oven to a baking temperature of 375°F. Cut chicken into serving-sized pieces, rinse, and pat dry. Mix flour, salt, pepper, and lemon peel. Coat chicken with seasoned flour, reserving 1 tablespoon. Heat butter and oil in a large, heavy skillet and fry chicken quickly until nicely browned all over. Remove chicken to a shallow Pyrex baking dish sprayed with vegetable oil. Pour fat from skillet. Blend cider, honey, and reserved tablespoon of flour and add to skillet with apple, peach, and raisins. Cook until mixture thickens slightly. Pour over chicken and bake, vented in position 1, for 1–1¼ hours, or until chicken is fork-tender.

COOK'S NOTES:

Easy Duckling A L'Orange

SERVES 4.

Preheat cast-iron oven to a baking temperature of 350°F. Sprinkle duckling pieces lightly with seasonings. Place pieces, skin side down, directly on baking rack in cast-iron oven. Roast, unvented, for 20 minutes. Vent in position 1 and continue roasting for 1 hour. Quickly remove duck from oven, putting cover back on tightly to recover heat as quickly as possible. Place duckling in a lightly oiled round baking dish, skin side up; return to oven and roast, vented in position 1, for 40 minutes. Working as quickly as possible, brush with half the marmalade. Return cover, and roast 15 minutes longer in position 1. Glaze with remaining marmalade and roast in position 1 an additional 30–45 minutes, moving venting to position 2 for last 15 minutes.

4½–5-pound duckling, cut into quarters
Salt and pepper to taste
Garlic powder to taste (optional)
1½ cups orange marmalade

HINTS: It is possible to shorten the cooking time as much as 30 minutes if you can increase the heat source for about 5 minutes following each removal of the oven's cover and then return the heat source to the proper setting to maintain a baking temperature of 350°F. It is easier to cook and serve this recipe and the flavor of the marmalade seems to penetrate the meat better when the duckling is quartered. Placing a piece of tinfoil or a foil pie plate on the bottom of the oven during the first part of the baking time helps to make cleanup easier.

COOK'S NOTES:

Roast Turkey Dinner

SERVES 4 GENEROUSLY.

I have tried several methods of roasting turkey on the stovetop, as well as several different types of pan, and the following method proved to be most successful. It gives a reasonable amount of browning as well as some crisping to the skin.

Vegetables
4 large potatoes
6 large carrots
Salt and pepper to taste
2 tablespoons butter

Peel potatoes and cut into 1-inch chunks. Scrape carrots and cut into small chunks. Use a square of tinfoil large enough to wrap each group of vegetables completely. Place vegetables in center of foil squares. Add salt and pepper and 1 tablespoon butter to each packet; wrap securely, folding over edges so bundles are well sealed and vegetables will steam in their own natural juices. Set aside until ready to add to turkey.

Turkey
8½-pound broiler turkey
2 cups Homemade Stuffing for Meat and Poultry, with sausage (p. 41)
Paprika to taste
Pepper to taste
½ cup melted butter
Salt to taste

Baking temperature should be maintained at 275°F. Place a cast-iron or heavy metal trivet with ½–¾-inch feet in a large agateware roaster that has been adjusted for venting according to directions on page 14. Place a shallow (no deeper than 1 inch) *aluminum* baking pan on trivet. Baking pan should be large enough to cover entire area under turkey. Place a roasting rack over baking pan (see sketch). Rinse turkey and pat very dry; this is important to browning process. Stuff turkey if desired, then rub all over with paprika and sprinkle with salt and pepper. Place turkey, breast side *down*, on roasting rack. Cover roaster and open all vent holes. At 275°F, you must plan on almost double the roasting time given in charts (about 6½ hours for an 8½-pound turkey), but this method is still best to have an evenly cooked turkey. Halfway through roasting time, turn turkey breast side up. Working quickly, insert meat thermometer as shown in sketch. Baste lightly with melted butter and add vegetable packets. Cover roaster, add stovetop thermometer, and fully vent. Continue roasting, being careful to adjust dampers on stove as necessary to maintain a roasting temperature of 275°F. It is easy for agateware to become too hot or too cool quickly. When turkey is done, meat thermometer should register

175–185°F, or drumstick should move freely in joint. (If turkey is small and not stuffed, you will have to depend on drumstick method of checking for doneness.) Remove turkey from roaster to a warm platter. Remove vegetable packets and drippings pan. Return vegetables to roaster, cover, and remove roaster from heat. Vegetables will stay hot till serving time this way. Return drippings pan to stovetop or scrape drippings, including brown parts that stick to pan, into a small, heavy saucepan and make gravy.

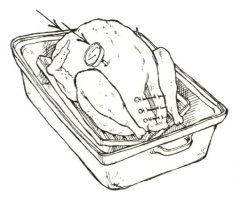

Placement of thermometer for stuffed turkey or chicken: put thermometer through side of bird into cavity and center of stuffing.

HINTS: If your bundles of vegetables are too big to slide in beside the turkey, make several smaller ones (divide butter) and put them all around the pan. On occasions when I don't feel like making stuffing, I peel a few small onions and stuff them into the cavity of the turkey right from the start. This flavors the turkey and provides an extra vegetable. If your roaster cover is not prepared for venting as shown in the sketch, you can place a skewer under the cover on one corner of the roasting pan to raise the cover slightly. It is a good idea to move the skewer to a different corner periodically for more even browning. This recipe should make a dinner for 4 with leftover turkey for another meal.

COOK'S NOTES:

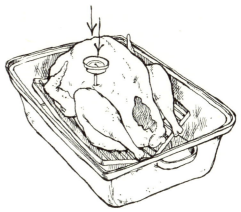

Placement of thermometer for turkey or chicken without stuffing: put thermometer straight down into large thigh muscle.

Sunday Supper Chicken

SERVES 4.

2 cups cooked broccoli, drained
1 cup cooked chicken slices
¼ teaspoon Homemade Poultry
    Seasoning (p. 42)
1¼ cups Velouté Sauce I (p. 36)
½ cup mayonnaise
2 teaspoons lemon juice
½ teaspoon salt
¼ teaspoon pepper
½ cup grated cheddar cheese
½ cup Buttered Crumb Topping
    (p. 40), using cracker crumbs

Preheat cast-iron oven to a baking temperature of 375°F. Place broccoli in a 9-inch deep cake plate sprayed with vegetable oil. Top with chicken slices. Mix remaining ingredients except cheese and crumb topping and pour over chicken. Bake, vented in position 1, for 30 minutes. Top with cheese and then with cracker crumb topping and bake in position 1 an additional 20 minutes.

HINTS: This recipe can be cooked in a baking dish that is smaller in diameter. Allow extra time, in venting position 1, for the dish to be bubbling all through before adding cheese and crumb topping. Soup purées that make a good sauce for this dish are Cream of Chicken Soup (p. 50), Cream of Mushroom Soup (p. 60), and Corn and Ham Chowder (p. 54).

Quick and Easy Chicken Casserole

SERVES 4.

1½ cups cooked chicken, diced
¾ cup mayonnaise
6 green tail onions, sliced thin
½ teaspoon salt
Dash pepper
1½ teaspoons Worcestershire
    sauce
⅛ teaspoon hot pepper sauce
¾ cup Buttered Crumb Topping
    (p. 40), using bread crumbs
Paprika
Fresh parsley, chopped

Preheat cast-iron oven to a baking temperature of 375°F. Combine chicken, mayonnaise, onions, and seasonings. Turn mixture into a 1-quart Pyrex baking dish sprayed with vegetable oil. Top with crumb topping and sprinkle with paprika and parsley. Bake, vented in position 1, for 25–30 minutes.

HINTS: Leftover turkey may be substituted for chicken in this recipe.

COOK'S NOTES:

Turkey Chow Mein

12 CUPS

Stir-fry turkey, onions, celery, green pepper, and mush-rooms for 5 minutes in hot bacon drippings in a large wok or heavy cast-iron Dutch oven. Add broth, Chinese cabbage, bean sprouts, water chestnuts, bamboo shoots, seasonings, brown sugar, and soy sauce. Bring to a boil. Mix cornstarch with water and stir in immediately. Cook, stirring constantly, just until thickened. (Occasionally you might need extra cornstarch.) Remove from heat immediately and cover. Let stand 15 minutes to blend flavors. Hot sauce will continue cooking vege-tables until they are just tender-crisp. *Do not overcook vegetables.* Serve with crisp egg noodles and additional soy sauce.

HINTS: This recipe will serve 6 people generously if it's the only entrée. However, if you are serving a Chinese meal including several other dishes such as Chinese Egg Rolls (p. 126), Fried Rice (p. 127), Sweet and Sour Rabbit (p. 103), Baked Spareribs with Sweet and Sour Sauce (p. 39), or Stir-fried Beef and Broccoli (p. 74), this turkey chow mein will serve at least 12. You may substitute regular cabbage for the Chinese cabbage, Jerusalem artichokes for the water chestnuts, and white turnips, sliced thin, for the bamboo shoots. When using these vegetables, add them at the early stir-fry stage of cooking.

4 cups cooked turkey, diced
4 large onions, sliced
2 cups celery, cut into ¾-inch chunks
1 large green pepper, cut into thin strips
1 cup sliced mushrooms
6 tablespoons bacon drippings
4 cups rich turkey or chicken stock (see HINT p. 33)
½ head Chinese cabbage or bok choy, sliced coarsely
2 cups bean sprouts
1 cup sliced water chestnuts
1 cup sliced bamboo shoots
1 tablespoon salt
¼ teaspoon pepper
3 tablespoons brown sugar
4 tablespoons good soy sauce or tamari
½ cup cornstarch
6 tablespoons cold water
4–6 cups Chinese egg noodles

COOK'S NOTES:

Rabbit and Pork Pie

TWO 9-INCH PIES OR ONE 10-INCH DEEP-DISH PIE

I have adapted this pie from a very old recipe that called for a rich forcemeat filling. It is more work than the average recipe in this book, but I have used a less complicated substitute for the forcemeat. This pie is so delicious that I feel certain you'll find it well worth the effort.

Rabbit
2–2½-pound rabbit
¼ cup butter
½ cup Rich Chicken Stock (p. 33)
½ teaspoon salt
½ teaspoon Homemade Poultry Seasoning (p. 42)

Cut rabbit into serving-sized pieces. Pack pieces into a bean pot, Mason jar, or covered dish of any kind that can withstand boiling temperatures. (Crock-Pot owners, see Hints at end of recipe.) Add butter, chicken stock, and seasonings to container; cover and place on a rack in a large, heavy kettle. Pour boiling water in kettle to at least three-fourths the height of container holding rabbit. Cover kettle and keep water simmering several hours or overnight. Your aim is to gently steam rabbit in a small amount of rich broth so as to release its juices and make it tender without drying meat. When rabbit is cooked, remove it from container. Drain rabbit broth and reserve. Remove meat from bones in large pieces; cover and set aside. Discard bones and prepare pork pâté.

At this point preheat cast-iron oven to a baking temperature of 375°F.

Pork Pâté
1 pound ground pork
1 finely diced shallot
1 medium onion, diced fine
1 teaspoon salt
¼ teaspoon pepper
1 teaspoon Homemade Poultry Seasoning (p. 42)
1 large potato

Brown pork, shallot, and onion in a heavy *ungreased* skillet; add seasonings and 2 tablespoons of reserved rabbit broth. Simmer for 10 minutes. Drain pork mixture; cover meat and set aside. Skim excess fat from juices and return juices to remaining rabbit broth. Cook potato until tender; mash fine with a fork. (You should have at least 1 cup.) Mix potato with pork mixture to form a stiff pâté. Adjust seasonings; pâté should be highly flavored with salt, pepper, and poultry seasoning.

Gravy
Reserved rabbit broth
About 6 tablespoons flour

Measure reserved broth and place in a blender or food processor with 3 tablespoons of flour for each cup of liquid. (There will be about 2 cups of broth.) Blend until smooth. Pour into skillet that pork was cooked in and heat stirring constantly, until thickened. Adjust seasonings.

Line two 8-inch or one 10-inch deep-dish Pyrex pie plate with crust. Press pork pâté onto crust and place a layer of cooked rabbit on top of pâté. Top with gravy. Put top crust in place and brush with beaten egg. Roll out trimmings and cut small round bunny faces and pointed ears for decoration. Put faces and ears on top crust and brush these with beaten egg. Make eyes and mouth with small whole peppercorns, to be discarded when pie is eaten. Cut steam vents and bake, vented in position 1, for 1 hour for 8-inch pies and for about 1¼ hours for 10-inch deep-dish pie.

HINTS: This pie is delicious served hot, but it is equally delicious at room temperature, making it ideal to serve at a buffet dinner. It also freezes exceptionally well. To bake, place the frozen *unbaked* pie in the preheated oven, covered with foil. Bake, vented in position 1, for 30 minutes. Remove foil from the pie, and bake 1 hour longer. The rabbit can be successfully prepared by placing all the ingredients in a Crock-Pot on the low setting overnight. This steam-cooking method gives such a deliciously rich gravy that it would make a wonderful fricasseed rabbit. Grape or currant jelly as a relish enhances rabbit pie.

Piecrust
2 recipes Rich Piecrust dough for
9-inch double-crust pie (p. 45)
1 beaten egg
Small whole peppercorns

COOK'S NOTES:

Rabbit, Chicken, or Turkey in Wine Sauce

SERVES 4.

Sauce

2 tablespoons each: diced onion,
    celery, and carrot
1 tablespoon butter
½ teaspoon dried tarragon
    leaves
⅛ teaspoon pepper
½ teaspoon salt
½ cup Rich Chicken Stock (p. 33)
1 cup French Colombard wine
1½ cups cooked potatoes, diced

Meat and Vegetables

1 cup fresh new peas
2 tablespoons water
6 scallions, sliced thin (include
    some of the green)
2 tablespoons butter
2 cups cooked rabbit, chicken, or
    turkey meat, diced
½ cup cooked mushrooms,
    drained
½ cup heavy cream

Sauté onion, celery, and carrot in butter in a heavy 2-quart saucepan until limp but not brown. Add seasonings, chicken stock, and wine. Bring to a boil and boil 10 minutes. Put potatoes in a blender or food processor and add wine mixture. Purée until velvety smooth. Set sauce aside.

Cook new peas with water in a heavy saucepan with a snug-fitting cover until just tender. *Do not drain*. Rinse saucepan you made sauce in and sauté scallions in butter until tender. Add meat, mushrooms, peas, and wine sauce. Reheat until meat has heated through and sauce is piping hot. Stir in cream and reheat again, being careful not to boil, or cream will curdle. Serve on patty shells, crisp toast points, or rice.

HINTS: This recipe also makes a very good filling and sauce for crepes. It freezes beautifully. Reheat in the top of a double boiler, stirring often. Add additional wine for flavor if necessary. Frozen peas can be substituted for the new garden peas, but they haven't got quite the same fresh flavor.

COOK'S NOTES:

Rabbit and Ham in Wine Custard

SERVES 6–8.

Preheat cast-iron oven to a baking temperature of 375°F. Melt butter in a heavy skillet and sauté parsley, scallions, and mushrooms for 2 minutes. Add rabbit, ham, and seasonings, stirring to mix ingredients. Add vermouth and boil rapidly until wine is almost completely evaporated. Pour meat mixture into a greased 2-quart casserole. Beat egg yolks lightly with a fork and add to cream. Pour cream mixture over meat mixture and stir to mix. Sprinkle with Parmesan and paprika. Bake, unvented, for 10 minutes. Vent in position 1 and bake 15 minutes more. Remove oven from heat source and move venting to position 3. Leave casserole in oven for 10 minutes, then remove and let stand at room temperature 5–10 minutes before serving. Top of casserole should have a firm custardy consistency; center should be like a creamy custard sauce.

HINTS: This casserole, though rich, has a very delicate flavor; it should not be served with any dish that has a strong taste. A fresh salad and hot rolls would complete the meal.

¼ cup butter
2 tablespoons fresh parsley, chopped fine
5 tablespoons sliced scallions or shallots
1 cup fresh or frozen mushrooms, sliced
3 cups cooked boneless rabbit, cut into bite-sized pieces
1 cup cooked ham, cut into bite-sized pieces
1 teaspoon salt
¼ teaspoon pepper
1 teaspoon dried tarragon leaves
1 cup dry vermouth
4 egg yolks
2 cups light cream
¼ cup grated Parmesan cheese
Paprika

COOK'S NOTES:

Fried Rabbit or Chicken

SERVES 4.

2 cups all-purpose flour
½ teaspoon baking powder
1 teaspoon sugar
2 teaspoons dried parsley flakes
2 teaspoons salt
1 teaspoon garlic powder
1½ teaspoons dried oregano
1½ teaspoons dried basil
1 egg
¼ cup milk
2–2½-pound fryer rabbit or
   chicken, cut into pieces
Oil for cooking (preferably
   peanut oil)

Stir 1 cup of the flour, baking powder, sugar, and seasonings together until thoroughly mixed. Blend egg and milk until smooth. Rinse rabbit or chicken and pat dry. Dip first in remaining cup of plain flour, dusting off excess, then in egg mixture, and finally in seasoned flour. Heat 1 inch of cooking oil in a large cast-iron skillet until hot (380°F). Fry meat until browned on both sides. Cover skillet and continue frying for 20 minutes, turning once. Uncover and cook 10 minutes longer to crisp coating.

HINTS: Larger rabbits and chickens can be fried this way if they have first been parboiled until barely tender. They taste best if cooled in their broth before frying.

COOK'S NOTES:

Sweet and Sour Rabbit

SERVES 4–6.

This is an especially good way to make use of the large pieces of white meat from older rabbits culled from your stock. (See HINTS, p. 67.)

Preheat cast-iron oven to a baking temperature of 350°F. Combine all ingredients except sweet and sour sauce in a 1½-quart Pyrex baking dish; heat sauce and pour over. Bake, unvented, for 30 minutes. Vent in position 2 and bake an additional 30 minutes. Serve with Fried Rice (p. 127) or plain rice.

HINTS: If you do not have tiny onions, use larger ones cut into quarters and parboil for 3 minutes before adding them to the dish.

3 cups cooked rabbit meat, cut into bite-sized pieces
½ large sweet red pepper, cut into bite-sized pieces
½ large sweet green pepper, cut into bite-sized pieces
1 cup celery, cut into bite-sized chunks
8 tiny whole onions
1 cup pineapple chunks, drained
1 cup cooked bean sprouts, drained
1½ cups Sweet and Sour Sauce (p. 39)

COOK'S NOTES:

Seafood and Fish

Seafood Thermidor Pie

SERVES 6 GENEROUSLY.

Lobster thermidor, usually served in the excavated shell of the lobster, is very expensive. The following recipe is just as tasty; in fact, it's hard to tell that half of the seafood is fillet of sole or cod. The unusual piecrust lends a new dimension to this acknowledged "classic" of the seafood culinary arts. Best of all, it will serve 6 generously for less than the cost of 2 servings of the original recipe.

Crust

½ cup potatoes, mashed
  without *milk, butter, or
  seasonings*
1½ cups all-purpose unbleached
  flour
3 tablespoons butter
1 egg
⅓ cup grated Parmesan cheese
1 very finely minced shallot
1 teaspoon fresh parsley,
  chopped
1 teaspoon salt
Pinch garlic powder
2 dashes hot pepper sauce

Preheat cast-iron oven to a baking temperature of 375°F. Combine all ingredients and mix thoroughly; a food processor does nicely. Divide dough in half and roll out one half onto a lightly floured board. (Freeze remaining dough for another pie.) Fit crust into a 9-inch Pyrex pie plate sprayed with vegetable oil and form a small rim around top edge. Bake, vented in position 1, for 20 minutes. Remove partially baked crust from oven and fill with seafood mixture.

Seafood Mixture

½ cup fresh or frozen
  mushrooms, sliced
7 tablespoons butter
4 tablespoons all-purpose flour
1 egg yolk
1 cup light cream
¼ cup cooking sherry
¼ teaspoon salt
¼ teaspoon garlic powder

Sauté mushrooms in 4 tablespoons of the butter in a medium-sized heavy saucepan until tender. Sprinkle in flour and stir thoroughly to blend. Beat egg yolk with cream, sherry, and seasonings; add to saucepan. Cook, stirring constantly, until thickened. Stir in lobster and sole or cod and cook 1 minute. Mix Parmesan and bread crumbs with a fork. Melt remaining 3 tablespoons of butter, then toss with crumb mixture. Pour seafood mixture into partially baked piecrust, top with crumb mixture, and bake, vented in position 2, for 20–30 minutes; sauce should bubble slightly all over. Let stand 5 minutes before serving.

HINTS: Can't afford lobster? Use tuna. Believe me, tuna never had it so good! Other fish and seafood such as sole, halibut, pollock, shrimp, and crabmeat can be used in combination.

Dash red cayenne pepper
⅛ teaspoon paprika
1 cup cooked lobster, cut into
  bite-sized pieces
1 cup poached fillet of sole or cod,
  cut into bite-sized pieces
¼ cup grated Parmesan cheese
⅔ cup dry bread crumbs

COOK'S NOTES:

Scalloped Clams with Mushrooms

SERVES 4.

½ cup cooked mushrooms,
  drained
½ cup diced onion
3 tablespoons butter
3 tablespoons all-purpose flour
¼ teaspoon salt
Dash or two cayenne pepper
¾ cup milk
13 ounces minced clams, drained
½ cup Buttered Crumb Topping
  (p. 40), using crackers

Preheat cast-iron oven to a baking temperature of 375°F. Sauté drained mushrooms and onion in butter until onion is tender but not brown. Blend flour, salt, cayenne, and milk in a blender or food processor, or shake in a quart jar with a cover until blended. Add milk mixture to onion mixture and cook, stirring constantly, until thick and bubbly. Stir in clams and pour into a 1-quart Pyrex casserole dish sprayed with vegetable oil. Bake, vented in position 1, for 15 minutes, add crumb topping, move venting to position 2, and bake 15 minutes longer.

Scalloped Corn and Clams

SERVES 4–6.

About 3 slices dry bread
3 eggs
13 ounces minced clams (drain
  and reserve broth)
½ cup diced onion
½ cup diced green pepper
2 tablespoons butter
2 cups thick cream-style corn
1 teaspoon salt
¼ teaspoon pepper
Dash hot pepper sauce
¾ cup Buttered Crumb Topping
  (p. 40), using crackers

Preheat cast-iron oven to a baking temperature of 350–375°F. Break bread into small pieces and put into a blender or food processor with eggs and 2 tablespoons of the reserved clam broth; blend until smooth. Sauté onion and pepper in butter until limp but not brown. Mix corn, drained clams, sautéed vegetables, and egg mixture with seasonings in a bowl until well blended. Turn into a 1½-quart Pyrex casserole dish sprayed with vegetable oil. Bake, vented in position 2, for 35–45 minutes or until table knife inserted near center comes out clean. Quickly top with crumb topping and bake, vented in position 3, 15 minutes longer.

HINTS: Freeze remaining clam broth in a small jar to be used in fish chowders or sauces.

COOK'S NOTES:

Shrimp Cauliflower Supreme

SERVES 6.

It is very important to use fresh cauliflower for this recipe. Frozen cauliflower cooks up too watery to be used successfully.

Preheat cast-iron oven to a baking temperature of 375°F. Steam cauliflower or cook in a minimum of salted water until just tender-crisp; drain and set aside. Sauté mushrooms and scallions in butter until barely tender. Blend cream sauce, flour, seasonings, and cheeses in a blender or food processor until smooth. Combine with drained cauliflower and shrimp in a 2-quart Pyrex casserole dish sprayed with vegetable oil. Bake, unvented, for 15 minutes. Vent in position 1 and bake 20 minutes longer. Working quickly, sprinkle crumb topping and paprika over casserole. Move venting to position 2 and bake an additional 20 minutes. Let stand 5 minutes before serving.

HINTS: I have found that the 6-ounce packages of small frozen cooked salad shrimp are the least expensive to buy and every bit as acceptable as the larger shrimp. Since they are already cooked, just pour cold water over them, let stand for 1 minute, and separate the pieces. Soup purées that make a good sauce for this dish are Tuna Chowder (p. 49), Corn and Ham Chowder (p. 54), Crabmeat Bisque (p. 48), and Cream of Mushroom Soup (p. 60).

3 cups fresh cauliflower florets (about 1 large head)
1 cup cooked mushrooms, drained
5 diced scallions (include some of the green)
1 tablespoon butter
1½ cups Thick Cream Sauce (p. 36)
4 tablespoons all-purpose flour
1 teaspoon salt
½ teaspoon pepper
⅛ teaspoon hot pepper sauce
6 ounces American-type processed cheese
¼ cup grated Parmesan cheese
6 ounces small cooked salad shrimp, shelled and deveined
¾ cup Buttered Crumb Topping (p. 40)
Paprika to taste

COOK'S NOTES:

Seafood Casserole

SERVES 6.

1 clove garlic, minced fine
2 tablespoons diced onion
½ cup fresh or frozen
   mushrooms, sliced
½ cup diced sweet red pepper
2 tablespoons butter
3 cups Fish Sauce (p. 37) or thick
   soup purée
1 cup cooked crabmeat
¾ cup cooked shrimp
¾ teaspoon salt
⅛ teaspoon red cayenne pepper
3 cups cooked macaroni
1 cup grated cheddar cheese
⅔ cup Buttered Crumb Topping
   (p. 40)

Preheat cast-iron oven to a baking temperature of 375°F. In a heavy skillet, sauté garlic, onion, mushrooms, and red pepper in butter until limp but not brown. Add fish sauce and heat until bubbly. Remove pan from heat, stir in seafood, seasonings, and macaroni, then pour into a 2-quart Pyrex casserole dish sprayed with vegetable oil. Bake, unvented for 30 minutes. Working quickly, sprinkle on cheese and then crumb topping. Vent in position 2 and bake an additional 20 minutes.

HINTS: Soup purées that make a good sauce for this dish are Tuna Chowder (p. 49), Crabmeat Bisque (p. 48), Cream of Mushroom Soup (p. 60), and Corn and Ham Chowder (p. 54).

COOK'S NOTES:

Onion Clam Quiche

SERVES 6.

Most quiches were created to be served at ladies' luncheons and events of this nature, and as such they should be light, delicate, and delicious. Muenster and Parmesan cheese combine with a generous quantity of onions and clams to give this quiche a more robust flavor that will appeal to those with hearty appetites. Served warm with a salad and hot rolls, perhaps some chilled white wine or a tall glass of icy-cold beer (one of the light varieties), this offering is fine company fare.

Preheat cast-iron oven to a baking temperature of 375°F. Sauté onions in butter until limp but not brown. Drain clams, reserving 4 tablespoons broth, and set aside. Lightly beat separated egg white with fork and brush unbaked piecrust lightly to seal. (See tips on piecrust, p. 43.) Put balance of egg white with remaining ingredients except chives and paprika into a blender or food processor and purée until smooth. If you haven't a blender or food processor, grate cheese very fine and beat all ingredients with an electric mixer until well blended. Mix clams with onions and spread over bottom crust. Pour egg-cheese mixture over onion mixture and sprinkle with chives and paprika. Bake, vented in position 2, for 40 minutes, or until a table knife inserted close to center comes out clean. Let stand 5–8 minutes for custard to set before serving.

2 large onions, sliced thin
2 tablespoons butter
½ cup minced clams, drained
4 eggs (separate 1)
Rich Piecrust dough for 9-inch double-crust pie (p. 45)
¼ cup grated Parmesan cheese
6 ounces muenster cheese, diced small or grated
½ teaspoon salt
¼ teaspoon pepper
⅛ teaspoon garlic powder
3 dashes hot pepper sauce
1 teaspoon finely chopped chives
Paprika

HINTS: With a little advance preparation, this quiche can even go on a picnic. Prepare the piecrust in the pie plate and wrap with plastic, then put the pie plate in the cooler along with Mason jars of the prepared fillings. Bake in the cast-iron oven over an open fire or a charcoal grill. Substitute crusty French bread for the hot rolls and serve with salad and wine or beer.

COOK'S NOTES:

Baked Haddock Fillet

SERVES 4.

2 tablespoons lemon juice
¾ teaspoon salt
½ teaspoon paprika
4 thick pieces haddock fillet
 (about 1½ pounds)
½ cup sliced onion
½ cup sliced green pepper
2 tablespoons butter
½ teaspoon grated lemon rind

Early in day, combine lemon juice, salt, and paprika in a shallow baking dish. Add fish fillets and turn once to coat with marinade. Cover tightly with plastic wrap and refrigerate 8 hours, turning once or twice. Remove from refrigerator 1 hour before dinner. Preheat cast-iron oven to a baking temperature of 375°F. In a medium-sized heavy skillet, sauté onion and green pepper in butter until limp but not brown. Place fish in a Pyrex pie plate sprayed with vegetable oil, cover with onion and green pepper, and sprinkle grated lemon rind over all. Bake, vented in position 1, for 20 minutes, or until haddock flakes easily with a fork.

Salmon Loaf

SERVES 6.

½ cup diced onion
⅓ cup diced green or red pepper
1 tablespoon fresh parsley,
 minced
3 tablespoons bacon drippings
1 cup milk
½ teaspoon salt
3 tablespoons flour
2 cups canned salmon, drained
 and with large bones removed
2 cups dried coarse bread crumbs
1 beaten egg
1 tablespoon lemon juice
⅛ teaspoon hot pepper sauce
 (optional)

Preheat cast-iron oven to a baking temperature of 375°F. In a heavy 1-quart saucepan, sauté onion, pepper, and parsley in bacon drippings until limp but not brown. Combine milk, salt, and flour in a blender or food processor and blend until smooth. Add to saucepan and cook, stirring constantly, until thickened. Mix with salmon, bread crumbs, egg, lemon juice, and hot pepper sauce, if desired. Turn into a 1½–2-quart Pyrex casserole dish sprayed with vegetable oil. Bake, vented in position 1, for 45–50 minutes. Top will be slightly brown, but center will still be soft and creamy. This loaf never comes out dry.

COOK'S NOTES:

Fillet of Sole Newburg

SERVES 4–6.

Poach fillet of sole in fish or chicken stock for just 3 minutes. With a slotted spoon, remove fish from stock to a bowl; cover and set aside. In a medium-sized heavy skillet, melt butter and stir in flour. Cook for a minute or two until mixture forms a smooth paste. *Do not brown.* Add cream all at once, stirring constantly. Cook over low to medium heat until sauce thickens and bubbles all over. Stir a small amount into beaten egg yolks, then return egg mixture to skillet and cook until thickened. Add fish, sherry, lemon juice, and salt. Reheat just until fish is completely cooked. Serve on patty shells or crisp toast points.

2 cups cooked fillet of sole, cut into 1-inch cubes
1½ cups Fish Stock (p. 34) or Rich Chicken Stock (p. 33)
6 tablespoons butter
3 tablespoons all-purpose flour
2 cups light cream
4 beaten egg yolks
3 tablespoons cooking sherry
2 teaspoons lemon juice
½ teaspoon salt

HINTS: For a company dinner, you could substitute cooked shrimp, lobster, or crabmeat for the sole, but I think the sole itself makes a very acceptable Newburg.

COOK'S NOTES:

Baked Fillet of Sole with Spinach

SERVES 4.

12 ounces fresh or frozen spinach
  (thawed if frozen)
1 pound fillet of sole, cut into
  serving-sized pieces
1 cup Fish Sauce (p. 37)
1 ½ tablespoons cooking sherry
½ cup grated Parmesan cheese
⅔ cup Buttered Crumb Topping
  (p. 40)
1 tablespoon fresh parsley,
  chopped fine
Paprika to taste
1 tablespoon grated lemon rind

Preheat cast-iron oven to a baking temperature of 375°F. If you're using fresh spinach, rinse and place in a large, heavy saucepan with just water that clings to leaves. Cover tightly and steam just until it is wilted. Drain fresh or thawed frozen spinach well, pressing out as much moisture as possible with back of a large spoon. Place spinach in an 8½- by 2-inch Pyrex baking dish sprayed with vegetable oil. Top with fish. Heat fish sauce with sherry and pour over fish; top with Parmesan and crumb topping. Sprinkle with parsley, paprika, and lemon rind. Bake, vented in position 2, for 25–30 minutes until fish flakes.

HINTS: Any mild-flavored fish fillets may be used instead of sole. Soup purées that make a good sauce for this dish are Crabmeat Bisque (p. 48), Tuna Chowder (p. 49), and Corn and Ham Chowder (p. 54).

COOK'S NOTES:

Batter-Fried Fish Fillets

SERVES 4.

Scorch flour by placing it in a heavy cast-iron skillet that is *not* greased. Place skillet over medium heat and stir flour constantly until it is the golden brown color of whole-wheat flour. Cool and mix with salt, pepper, and baking powder. Rinse fish fillets and pat dry. Blend lemon rind, egg, and milk until smooth; add dry ingredients and blend to make a smooth batter. Dip fish pieces in batter and deep-fry in hot peanut oil (375–385°F) until golden brown on both sides, about 5 minutes.

HINTS: Small cubes of fish fried according to this recipe make excellent hot hors d'oeuvres. Serve them with Hot Orange Mustard Sauce (p. 38) or Creamy Horseradish Sauce (p. 38).

1½ cups all-purpose flour
1 teaspoon salt
Dash pepper
1½ teaspoons double-acting baking powder
1 pound fish fillets (sole, haddock, halibut, cod, pollock)
1 teaspoon grated lemon rind
1 egg
1½ cups milk
Peanut oil for frying

Tuna Noodle Casserole

SERVES 4.

Preheat cast-iron oven to a baking temperature of 375°F. Cook egg noodles according to package directions and drain. Heat fish sauce until bubbly, then combine it with noodles, tuna, mushrooms, parsley, and seasonings in a 2-quart Pyrex casserole dish sprayed with vegetable oil. Bake, unvented, for 30 minutes. Working quickly, spread crumb topping over casserole. Vent in position 1 and bake 15 minutes longer.

HINTS: Homemade soup purées that make a good sauce for this dish are Corn and Ham Chowder (p. 54), Cream of Mushroom Soup (p. 60), Tuna Chowder (p. 49), Crabmeat Bisque (p. 48), and Cream of Celery Soup (p. 59).

6 ounces medium egg noodles
2 cups thick Fish Sauce (p. 37) or thick soup purée (see HINTS)
6½ ounces drained tuna fish
½ cup cooked mushrooms, drained and sliced
1 tablespoon fresh parsley, chopped fine
½ teaspoon salt
¼ teaspoon pepper
⅔ cup Buttered Crumb Topping (p. 40)

COOK'S NOTES:

Creamed Tuna with Peas

SERVES 4–6.

12 ounces drained tuna fish
2 cups cooked peas, drained
4 tablespoons bacon fat or butter
10 tablespoons all-purpose flour
1 teaspoon salt
¼ teaspoon pepper
4 cups milk

Place tuna and peas in a heavy 4-quart saucepan. Put bacon fat, flour, salt, pepper, and 2 cups of the milk in a blender or food processor and blend until smooth. Pour into pan with tuna and peas; add remaining milk. Bring to a boil and simmer 3–5 minutes, stirring constantly.

HINTS: This makes a very good and quick high-protein meal. Serve over baked potatoes, toast, biscuits, or even crisp Chinese egg noodles.

Tuna Rice Supper

SERVES 4.

½ cup sliced scallions (include some of the green)
¼ cup diced green pepper
2 tablespoons butter
6½ ounces drained tuna fish
2 cups cooked rice
1 tablespoon lemon juice
1 teaspoon salt
¼ teaspoon pepper
2 slightly beaten eggs
¾ cup milk
½ cup grated cheddar cheese
¾ cup Buttered Crumb Topping (p. 40)

Preheat cast-iron oven to a baking temperature of 375°F. In a small skillet, sauté scallions and green pepper in butter until tender. Combine with tuna, rice, lemon juice, seasonings, eggs, and milk in a 2-quart Pyrex casserole dish sprayed with vegetable oil. Bake, unvented, for 30 minutes. Working quickly, sprinkle grated cheese and then crumb topping over casserole. Bake, vented in position 1, for an additional 15 minutes. Move venting to position 2 and bake 15 minutes longer.

COOK'S NOTES:

Homemade Pasta

¾ POUND

Mix all-purpose flour with semolina and make it into a little mound on a clean surface. Make an indentation in center and put egg, egg white, olive oil, and salt in center. Working with your hands or a pasta fork, from outside in thoroughly mix dough, adding only enough drops of water for dough to hold together. Knead until smooth and elastic, or use a noodle maker according to directions. After kneading, let dough set for about 5 minutes, then roll it out into a very thin rectangle. Carefully roll dough like a jelly roll. Slice into desired widths with a sharp knife. Unroll strips and dry on a clean linen towel or on a noodle dry rack.

1 cup all-purpose unbleached flour
½ cup semolina flour (purchase in health food store)
1 egg
1 egg white
1 tablespoon olive oil
1 teaspoon salt

HINTS: You may make up large amounts of pasta at a time, but mix each batch separately to get a good quality noodle. Fresh homemade pasta cooks more quickly than commercially prepared dried pasta: 1 to 2 minutes in boiling salted water are sufficient.

Pasta Equivalents

Often a recipe will call for a number of cups of cooked pasta or rice, sending us scurrying for a box that might tell us how much to cook. The following chart gives a pretty accurate idea of the yield on most popular brands.

HINTS: To make a large amount of pasta for year round use, cover the dowels of your wood clothes dryer with waxed paper and dry the strips of pasta quickly near your wood or coal heater.

VARIETY	UNCOOKED	COOKED
Elbows	2 cups	4 cups
Spaghetti	2 cups	4 cups
Rotelle (spirals)	4 cups	4 cups
Farfalli (butterflies)	5 cups	4 cups
Shells (small)	2 cups	4 cups
Noodles (wide and regular)	6 cups	3½ cups
Noodles (fine)	5 cups	3½ cups
Raw rice	1 cup	3 cups
Precooked rice	1⅓ cups	3 cups

My Favorite Spaghetti Sauce ✓

ABOUT 5 CUPS

1 pound ground beef
1 large clove garlic, minced very
  fine
1 large onion, diced
2 tablespoons bacon fat or
  cooking oil
1 teaspoon crushed red pepper
1 tablespoon fresh oregano,
  chopped fine
2 tablespoons fresh basil,
  chopped fine
½ tablespoon fresh sweet
  marjoram, chopped fine
2 teaspoons salt
¼ teaspoon pepper
3 tablespoons honey
2 quarts canned tomatoes
12 ounces tomato paste

Brown beef, garlic, and onion in bacon fat until meat has lost its red color. Add remaining ingredients and simmer, uncovered, for 2 hours, stirring often.

HINTS: When fresh tomatoes are abundant in the summer, I blanch and peel 10 large ones to use in place of the canned tomatoes. This sauce is highly seasoned, so if you aren't sure you like a strong-flavored sauce, you can start by adding just half the amount of herbs called for, taste the sauce halfway through the cooking time, and add more at this time if you like.

COOK'S NOTES:

Mrs. Young's Pasta Sauce with Meatballs

SERVES 8.

Wet slices of bread, then do not squeeze all water out of them; leave slightly moist. Mix with remaining ingredients except oil and shape into 1-inch meatballs. Brown meatballs in oil in a large skillet. Remove from skillet as they brown and drain on paper towels. When all meatballs are browned, put in a covered container and refrigerate until needed. Reserve cooking oil in skillet for making sauce.

Brown garlic in reserved oil in skillet. Add remaining ingredients and heat sauce to boiling; lower heat and simmer, uncovered, for 1½ hours, until very thick. If sauce thickens too much before cooking time is up, add a little water. It's important to cook it long enough to develop flavor. Add meatballs and cook another hour. Make sure to stir often to prevent sauce from sticking and scorching.

HINTS: This recipe makes enough sauce for about 2 pounds of pasta. Serve with additional grated Parmesan-Romano cheese.

Meatballs
4 slices bread
1½ pounds ground beef
2 eggs
¼ cup grated
    Parmesan-Romano cheese
1 clove garlic, minced fine
1 teaspoon salt
¼ teaspoon pepper
¼ teaspoon crushed red pepper
½ teaspoon dried basil
¼ cup salad oil

Sauce
2 cloves garlic, minced
1½ teaspoons salt
¼ teaspoon pepper
¼ teaspoon crushed red pepper
1 teaspoon parsley
1 teaspoon dried basil
4 cups canned tomatoes
12 ounces tomato paste

COOK'S NOTES:

Pizza Crust

¾ *cup warm water*
  (110–115°F)
1 tablespoon dry yeast
1½ teaspoons sugar
1 teaspoon salt
1½ tablespoons oil
2 tablespoons gluten flour
2 cups all-purpose unbleached
  flour

Preheat cast-iron oven to a baking temperature of 375°F. Place warm water in a medium-sized bowl. Add yeast, sugar, salt, oil, and gluten flour. Stir to blend and let stand 2–3 minutes. Add ½ cup of the all-purpose flour. Beat well until smooth with an electric mixer or wooden spoon. Continue adding all-purpose flour until you have a very stiff dough, using your hands if necessary. Turn dough out onto a lightly floured board and knead until smooth and elastic, about 5 minutes. Place in a bowl sprayed with vegetable oil; spray top of dough with vegetable oil to prevent drying. Cover with a heavy towel and let rise until double in bulk. Punch down, turn out onto a lightly floured board. Knead 4–5 times to remove air bubbles. Divide into 2 or 3 pieces and let rest on board for 5 minutes while you prepare baking rack. Remove rack from cast-iron oven and cover snugly with heavy tinfoil: punch several holes in foil with a sharp fork and spray foil-covered rack with vegetable oil. Roll out balls of dough to fit rack. Cover other pieces of dough with a damp towel until needed. Bake crusts, one at a time, vented in position 2, for 5–8 minutes. They will feel quite firm, but will not be browned. At this point, you can go on to make Pizza (p. 119) or freeze crusts for later use. (Add 3–5 minutes to baking time of pizza when using frozen crusts.)

HINTS: If freezer space is a problem, freeze unbaked pieces of dough until needed. Remove from freezer 1–2 hours before baking and roll and bake as directed. Campers: take note of these easy homemade pizzas that you can make on a charcoal grill.

COOK'S NOTES:

Pizza Sauce

ABOUT 1 CUP

Put all ingredients in a small, heavy saucepan and simmer for about 20 minutes, if you use tomato sauce, or for 35–40 minutes, if you use tomato juice.

HINTS: When the woodstove is going on a chilly day in midwinter, take out some of the tomato sauce you made in the fall and cook up large batches of this sauce. It can then be either frozen or stored in the refrigerator if you have room. It will keep well for about 3 weeks in the refrigerator.

1 cup thick tomato sauce or 2 cups tomato juice
1 small onion, diced
1 tablespoon dried basil
1 teaspoon garlic powder
¼ teaspoon crushed red pepper
1 tablespoon honey
⅛ teaspoon pepper
Salt to taste

Pizza

ONE 8–10-INCH PIZZA

Preheat cast-iron oven to a baking temperature of 375–400°F. Brush crust lightly with half the salad oil and spread pizza sauce over crust, up to very edge. Add favorite toppings; cover with Parmesan and mozzarella cheeses and sprinkle remaining oil over top. Quickly slip pizza directly onto foil-covered baking rack in oven. Bake, vented in position 2, for about 10 minutes, until cheese is bubbly. If a very crispy crust is desired, move venting to position 3 for an additional 2–3 minutes.

HINTS: For a change, try cheddar cheese instead of mozzarella. For quick individual pizzas, use English muffins split in half.

1 partially baked 8–10-inch Pizza Crust (p. 118)
1½ tablespoons salad oil or olive oil
¼ cup Pizza Sauce (preceding recipe)
Choice of toppings: onions, green peppers, black olives, anchovies, mushrooms, shrimp, pepperoni, sausage
2 tablespoons grated Parmesan cheese
1½–2 ounces sliced or shredded mozzarella cheese

COOK'S NOTES:

Baked Macaroni with Basil and Cheese

SERVES 4.

2 cups uncooked macaroni
3 slices lightly buttered bread
½ cup finely chopped walnuts
¾ cup fresh basil leaves, packed
1 cup shredded cheddar cheese
  (4 ounces)
½ cup grated Parmesan cheese
1 teaspoon garlic powder
1 teaspoon salt
¼ teaspoon pepper
¾ cup melted butter

Preheat cast-iron oven to a baking temperature of 375°F. Cook macaroni according to package directions and drain. Break bread into a blender or food processor and crumb coarsely. Put crumbs in a small, heavy skillet and cook over high heat, stirring constantly, until crumbs become crisp and nicely browned. Remove from heat and stir in walnuts. Blend remaining ingredients in blender or food processor until smooth; add to macaroni and stir thoroughly to mix. Turn into a 2-quart Pyrex casserole dish sprayed with vegetable oil and top with crumb mixture. Bake, vented in position 2, until cheese is melted and casserole has heated through (about 40 minutes).

HINTS: This dish, with its distinct *pesto* flavor, has the advantage of lending itself well to advance preparation. It makes a very different dish to bring to a covered-dish supper. Dried basil may be used instead of fresh, but use only 3–4 tablespoons at most.

COOK'S NOTES:

Baked Macaroni and Cheese

SERVES 4.

Preheat cast-iron oven to a baking temperature of 375°F. Cook macaroni according to package directions and drain. Place in an 8½- by 2-inch Pyrex baking dish sprayed with vegetable oil. Place remaining ingredients except topping and garnish in a blender or food processor and blend until smooth. Pour over macaroni; stir to mix. Bake, unvented, for 30 minutes. Working quickly, add crumb topping and bake, vented in position 2, for another 30 minutes. Remove from oven and sprinkle with fresh parsley and paprika before serving.

1½ cups uncooked macaroni
6 ounces (1½ cups) grated
   cheddar cheese
¼ cup grated Parmesan cheese
¾ cup hot milk
½ small onion
2 tablespoons all-purpose flour
1 tablespoon butter
½ teaspoon salt
⅛ teaspoon pepper
⅛ teaspoon dry mustard
¾ cup Buttered Crumb Topping
   (p. 40)
2 tablespoons fresh parsley,
   chopped
Paprika

COOK'S NOTES:

Eggplant Parmesan

SERVES 4.

1 medium eggplant
Salt
½ cup cornmeal
1 cup grated Parmesan cheese
1 cup all-purpose flour
1 teaspoon garlic powder
1 teaspoon salt
¼ teaspoon pepper
4½ teaspoons dried sweet basil
1 egg
¼ cup milk
⅛ teaspoon hot pepper sauce
1 teaspoon onion powder
Oil for frying
1 cup tomato sauce
1 cup shredded mozzarella
  cheese

Preheat cast-iron oven to a baking temperature of 375°F. Peel and slice eggplant into ½-inch slices. Salt liberally on both sides and place on paper towels for 30 minutes, turning once at 15 minutes. Mix cornmeal, ½ cup of the Parmesan, and ½ cup of the flour. Add garlic powder, salt, pepper, and 3 teaspoons of the basil and mix until well blended. Combine egg, milk, hot pepper sauce, and onion powder until well blended. Rinse eggplant in cold water and pat dry with paper towels. Dip first in remaining ½ cup flour to coat, shake off excess, dip in egg mixture, then in cornmeal mixture. Coat well on both sides. Fry in hot fat until golden brown on both sides. Drain on paper towels, then place in a round Pyrex baking dish sprayed with vegetable oil, overlapping slices to fit all in. Top with remaining ½ cup Parmesan, then tomato sauce; sprinkle with remaining 1½ teaspoons basil and garlic powder to taste and finish with mozzarella. Bake, vented in position 2, for 30 minutes, until cheese has melted and is bubbly.

COOK'S NOTES:

Meatless Dishes

Noodles with Butter and Cheese

SERVES 4.

Beat butter until soft and fluffy. Add cream a little at a time while beating. Beat in ½ cup of the Parmesan. Serve at room temperature on fettucini noodles with remaining grated Parmesan.

HINTS: This makes a nice, quick summertime supper with a garden salad and fresh Italian bread.

¼ pound soft butter
¼ cup heavy cream
1 cup freshly grated Parmesan cheese
1 pound cooked fettucini noodles, drained
Salt and pepper to taste

COOK'S NOTES:

Puffy Cheese Omelet

SERVES 2–3.

Occasionally someone stops by at lunchtime on a day you had planned to use leftovers that can't be stretched. If your cast-iron oven has been on the wood or coal heater for a while (see HINTS, p. 16), this omelet is not only quick to make but it is delicious and looks like a golden cloud.

3 eggs, separated
¼ teaspoon cream of tartar
2 tablespoons cold water
¼ teaspoon salt
Dash pepper
2 tablespoons mayonnaise
3 ounces shredded cheddar
  cheese
Sprig fresh parsley for garnish

Preheat cast-iron oven to a baking temperature of 375°F. Beat egg whites with cream of tartar in a medium-sized bowl with a narrow bottom till stiff but not dry. In a second medium-sized bowl beat egg yolks, water, salt, pepper, and mayonnaise until thick and lemon colored. Gently fold yolks into whites until no more white is visible. Carefully turn egg mixture into an 8½- by 2-inch Pyrex baking dish sprayed with vegetable oil. Slip dish quickly into oven, vent in position 2, and bake 15 minutes. Working quickly, top omelet with shredded cheese and bake in position 2 for an additional 20 minutes, or until cheese is melted. Remove baking dish from oven and slip omelet onto a heated platter. Fold one half over other and tuck a sprig of fresh parsley under one side.

HINTS: Any other cheese may be substituted for the cheddar. You may also add other ingredients, such as crisp bacon pieces or chopped cooked chicken livers, or you may serve omelet with a tomato sauce. For a summer treat, add blanched, peeled, and sliced tomatoes before you top with cheese. To serve, do not fold; cut in wedges.

COOK'S NOTES:

Cheese and Onion Strata

SERVES 6.

Trim crust from 4 slices of the bread and cut in triangles; set aside, reserving trimmings. Cut remaining slices into large cubes. Sauté onions in butter until limp but not brown. Layer cubes of bread and bread trimmings with cheese and onions in a 2-quart Pyrex casserole dish sprayed with vegetable oil. Top with triangles of bread in a pretty pattern. Beat remaining ingredients except garnish and pour over bread. Refrigerate at least 8 hours or overnight. In morning, preheat cast-iron oven to a baking temperature of 350–375°F. Bring dish to room temperature before baking. Sprinkle top with paprika and chopped fresh parsley and bake, unvented, for 10 minutes. Vent in position 1 and bake for 40 minutes. Move venting to position 2 and bake an additional 20 minutes. Let stand 10 minutes before serving.

8 slices day-old bread
2 large onions, sliced very thin
2 tablespoons butter
6 ounces (1½ cups) thinly sliced
  Swiss cheese
4 eggs
2½ cups milk
1½ teaspoons salt
½ teaspoon prepared mustard
¼ teaspoon black pepper
Dash cayenne pepper
Dash paprika
2 tablespoons fresh parsley,
  chopped

HINTS: **Any other cheese may be substituted for the Swiss.**

COOK'S NOTES:

Chinese Egg Rolls

36 ROLLS

1 cup finely diced meat or seafood
½ cup finely chopped green
    onion
1 cup finely chopped celery
1½ cups finely chopped Chinese
    cabbage
1½ cups raw bean sprouts,
    chopped fine (do not use
    cooked sprouts)
3 tablespoons soy sauce
1 tablespoon salt
2 tablespoons brown sugar
2 tablespoons cornstarch
1-pound package wonton
    wrappers
Flour and water to seal
2 cups peanut oil

Combine first 8 ingredients in a heavy saucepan and cook for 5 minutes. Cool 30 minutes, then drain well. Sift cornstarch over drained mixture and stir well to incorporate. Let stand 5 minutes. Place 1 heaping teaspoon vegetable mixture in center of each wonton wrapper and fold according to sketch. Mix a paste of flour and water to seal rolls. Place rolls under damp towel until ready to fry. Fry in hot peanut oil until golden brown. Serve with Hot Orange Mustard Sauce (p. 38).

HINTS: Wonton wrappers may be purchased in most supermarkets today, as well as Oriental specialty stores. I prefer them to egg roll wrappers because they are crispier and freeze nicely. To reheat, fry *frozen cooked* egg rolls in hot peanut oil for 2–3 minutes. A food processor makes quick work of mincing the vegetables.

COOK'S NOTES:

WRAPPING EGG ROLLS

Bring one corner up over filling.

Bring left-hand corner to center.

Place filling in center of wonton wrapper.

Fold right-hand corner over first fold.

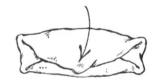
Fold top corner down snugly and seal with flour and water paste.

Fried Rice

SERVES 4.

Bring water, stock, 1 teaspoon of the salt, and onion powder to a boil in a heavy 2-quart saucepan. Add rice, return to a boil, and simmer, covered, for just 15 minutes (rice should be slightly underdone). Let stand, covered, until all water is absorbed. Meanwhile, fry bacon until crisp. Remove from pan with a slotted spoon and set aside. Over high heat, stir-fry green and red pepper, celery, and onions for just 2 minutes in hot bacon drippings. Remove vegetables with slotted spoon and set aside. Add salad oil (or additional bacon fat) to pan, add rice, and fry for 5 minutes until just slightly brown. While rice is frying, add remaining ½ teaspoon of the salt, pepper, soy sauce, and brown sugar to eggs and beat lightly in a cup or small bowl. Return bacon and fried vegetables along with mushrooms and bean sprouts to rice in pan. Mix well and fry for a minute or two to heat. Push rice and vegetables to one side of pan, add egg mixture, and cook, stirring constantly. When egg mixture is almost done, incorporate it into rice and mix well. Shut off heat and let stand a few minutes to blend flavors.

1 cup water
½ cup Rich Chicken Stock (p. 33)
1½ teaspoons salt
1 teaspoon onion powder
1 cup raw rice
4 slices diced bacon
¼ cup diced green pepper
¼ cup diced red pepper
½ cup diced celery
8–10 green tail onions (use green part) or 1 cup diced onion
4 tablespoons salad oil
¾ cup cooked mushrooms, drained
1 cup cooked bean sprouts, drained and rinsed
⅛ teaspoon pepper
2 teaspoons soy sauce
2 teaspoons brown sugar
2 eggs

HINTS: This recipe may be frozen and reheated, covered, in a hot oven. Stir once or twice while reheating in order to heat quickly and evenly; otherwise some of the reheated rice may become too soft.

COOK'S NOTES:

Country Kitchen Baked Beans

SERVES 6.

1 pound yellow eye beans
¼ teaspoon baking soda
1 teaspoon dry mustard
1 teaspoon salt
¼ teaspoon pepper
4 tablespoons prepared
    horseradish
¼ cup catsup
2 tablespoons light molasses
8 tablespoons brown sugar
4 small onions
6 slices bacon, cut in half

Soak beans overnight in triple their volume of water. In morning, preheat cast-iron oven to a baking temperature of 325°F. Drain, rinse, and put beans in a large kettle; cover with water and add baking soda. Bring to a boil and simmer, uncovered, about 1 hour, or until a bean can be pierced with a fork. Skim off foam that rises while cooking. Drain, rinse, and put into a greased 2-quart Pyrex casserole dish. Add remaining ingredients except onions and bacon; mix well. Fill baking dish with very hot water to come just to top of beans. Place whole onions on top and lay bacon slices over entire casserole. Bake, unvented, for 2 hours, then vent in position 1 and bake an additional 2½–3 hours. Move venting to position 2 and bake 30 minutes more, or until done. Add boiling water as necessary, but do it quickly so as not to lose heat.

HINTS: When you buy dry beans in the supermarket, there is no way to find out how old they are, and it seems to me that in the past year I have bought some that were so old they had become petrified. These beans take forever to cook; sometimes it is impossible to get them tender. If you don't grow your own dry beans, I would suggest that you try to buy them from a food cooperative or a natural food store. Prices are rarely higher, and you stand a better chance of getting beans that are not over a year old.

COOK'S NOTES:

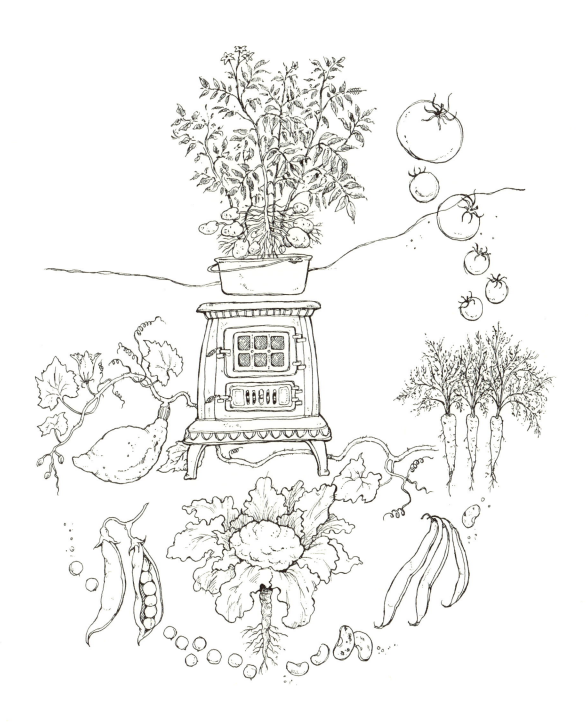

Vegetables

Marinated Fresh Vegetables

5 CUPS (ENOUGH FOR 12 CUPS OF VEGETABLES)

Marinade
1 cup cider vinegar
3 cups salad oil
¼ cup honey
1 teaspoon dry mustard
1 teaspoon paprika
½ teaspoon salt
¼ teaspoon pepper
6 cloves garlic, minced
½ cup prepared horseradish

Blend thoroughly in a blender or food processor.

Vegetables to Marinade
Artichoke hearts
Asparagus
Broccoli
Carrots
Cauliflower
Celery
Green beans
Green peppers
*Kidney beans (cooked until
    tender)*
Mushrooms
Small onions
Sweet red peppers
Yellow beans
Zucchini

Choose a variety of vegetables and clean them well. Peel when necessary and cut into bite-sized chunks. Steam or cook in small amount of water until barely tender. (They should still have some crunch.) Drain, place in a large bowl, and cover with marinade while still warm. When all vegetables have been cooked and added to bowl, stir well to mix vegetables and marinade and pack into jars. Seal well. Refrigerate and let stand at least 24 hours before serving. They will keep a month or more.

HINTS: This is a wonderful salad all year round, but it's a special treat in midwinter when good quality fresh salad vegetables are scarce and their price is dear. This recipe is one way to use many root crops that have been stored in the root cellar over the winter. Serve a bowl of these crisp, bright, tasty vegetables as hors d'oeuvres for a nice change. Be sure to include some of the brightly colored vegetables.

COOK'S NOTES:

Potatoes Anna

SERVES 6–8.

This time-honored way of preparing potatoes turns a simple supper of leftover cold roast or poultry into a company meal.

Preheat cast-iron oven to a baking temperature of 375°F. Peel potatoes and slice thin. Butter an 8½- by 2-inch Pyrex baking dish. Overlap a layer of potatoes in a swirl pattern in bottom of dish. Stand more potato slices on end all around side of dish. Sprinkle first layer with salt and pepper and dot with butter. Continue layering potatoes, sprinkling each layer with salt and pepper and dotting with butter, until dish is filled. Bake, unvented, for 30 minutes. Vent in position 2 and bake an additional 30 minutes, or until potatoes are fork-tender in center. Invert on a serving plate; outside should be brown and crisp and inside should be tender and buttery.

12–14 small potatoes (about 1½ inches in diameter)
Salt and pepper to taste
Butter

Baked Vegetables

SERVES 4.

To bake vegetables along with potatoes, take 1 pound any fresh vegetable cut into 1–2-inch pieces. Place vegetables in center of a large square of foil. Add 1 tablespoon butter and salt and pepper. Bring foil up around vegetables and twist top to seal. Vegetables will steam in their own juices and will taste very fresh. Carrots and squash will be very sweet. Bake along with potatoes for 1 hour, or with roasts for 1½–2 hours.

HINTS: A drying rack suspended from the ceiling over the heater dries everything from herbs to fruits and vegetables.

COOK'S NOTES:

Baked Potatoes

SERVES 4.

4 large baking potatoes

Preheat cast-iron oven to a baking temperature of 375°F. Scrub potatoes well and pierce in 1 or 2 places to prevent bursting. Bake, unvented, for 10 minutes. Vent in position 1 and bake for 1–1½ hours more. Turn once halfway through baking time if you would like to have crispy skins.

HINTS: Old potatoes bake in about 1 hour and 10 minutes; new potatoes bake in about 1½ hours. Potatoes may be baked along with roasts, because roasts are cooked at lower temperatures; however, you must plan on adding the potatoes 2 hours before roast is to be done.

Seasoned Potato Slices

SERVES 4.

4 large potatoes, scrubbed but
  unpeeled
5½ tablespoons salad oil
2½ tablespoons cider vinegar
1 teaspoon honey
½ teaspoon paprika
½ teaspoon garlic powder
½ teaspoon onion powder
¼ teaspoon dried sweet basil
¼ teaspoon dried oregano
Salt and pepper to taste

Steam potatoes over 1 inch of boiling salted water until barely tender. Meanwhile, make a marinade of remaining ingredients except salt and pepper. While still hot, cut potatoes into ½-inch slices. Place slices in a shallow Pyrex pie plate and pour marinade over them. Let stand at least 1 hour; longer is even better. Turn occasionally. At dinnertime, place potato slices directly on a hot grill or in a very hot, lightly greased heavy skillet and cook about 15–20 minutes, until potatoes are golden brown on both sides. Season with salt and pepper.

COOK'S NOTES:

Green Bean Casserole

SERVES 4–6.

This is a homemade version of a popular recipe using commercially prepared soup and onion rings. Though this recipe takes a little longer to put together, I think you will find it superior in taste to the quicker version.

Preheat cast-iron oven to a baking temperature of 375°F. Sauté mushrooms in butter until tender. Place in a blender or food processor with cream sauce, sherry, cayenne pepper, black pepper, and salt. Purée until smooth and set aside. Prepare onion rings. Heat sauce. Put a layer of green beans in an 8½- by 2-inch Pyrex baking dish sprayed with vegetable oil; add a layer of onion rings; top with half the sauce. Repeat, reserving last layer of onion rings for later. Bake, vented in position 2, for 30 minutes, or until bubbly. Quickly add remaining onion rings, move venting to position 3, and bake an additional 20–30 minutes.

½ cup fresh or frozen mushrooms, sliced
2 tablespoons butter
1 recipe Thick White Sauce (p. 36)
1 tablespoon cooking sherry
Dash cayenne pepper
¼ teaspoon black pepper
½ teaspoon salt
1 recipe Fried Onion Rings (following recipe)
4 cups cooked whole green beans, drained

HINTS: Soup purées that make a good sauce for this dish are Cream of Mushroom Soup (p. 60) and Corn and Ham Chowder (p. 54).

HINTS: Cook fresh vegetables in a small amount of water, or steam them on a steamer rack and save drained juices as well as those from canned vegetables that do not have an overpowering flavor. Add them to a plastic jug in the freezer as they come along, until it's time to make a soup such as American-style Minestrone (p. 55). These juices make soup more nourishing and flavorful.

COOK'S NOTES:

Fried Onion Rings

ABOUT 3 CUPS, PACKED LOOSE

2 medium sweet onions, sliced
 thin
Cold milk
1 egg
1 cup flour
2 teaspoons double-acting
 baking powder
1 teaspoon salt
¼ teaspoon pepper
Peanut oil for frying

Separate onion slices into rings, put in a small bowl, and cover with cold milk. Let stand 30 minutes. Drain well, reserving ¼ cup milk. Pat onion rings dry with paper towels. Blend egg and reserved onion milk. Mix flour with baking powder, salt, and pepper. Coat onion rings with flour mixture, then with egg mixture, and again with flour mixture. Heat 1½–2 inches of peanut oil to 375°F in a heavy cast-iron Dutch oven. Add onion rings one at a time (do not fry more than will fit in one layer at a time); turn once until golden brown. Drain on paper towels.

HINTS: These onion rings complement any pan-broiled meats and are an excellent side dish to be served with Batter-fried Fish Fillets (p. 113).

Cabbage Casserole

SERVES 4.

3 cups cooked cabbage, chopped
 and drained well
1½ cups Thick White Sauce
 (p. 36)
1 cup grated American cheese
1 teaspoon salt
⅛ teaspoon pepper
¾ cup Buttered Crumb Topping
 (p. 40)

Preheat cast-iron oven to a baking temperature of 375°F. Put cooked cabbage in a greased 8½- by 2-inch baking dish. Heat white sauce in a small saucepan until bubbly. Remove pan from heat and stir cheese, salt, and pepper into sauce. Pour over cabbage and stir to mix. Bake, unvented for 15 minutes. Working quickly, top cabbage mixture with crumb topping and bake, vented in position 2, for 20 minutes.

HINTS: For a more highly flavored dish, puréed Cabbage Soup (p. 52) may be substituted for the white sauce.

COOK'S NOTES:

Baked Stuffed Onions

Preheat cast-iron oven to a baking temperature of 375°F. Parboil onions 10–12 minutes; cool, reserving ½ cup of the onion water. Fry sausage and pour off all but 2 tablespoons of the sausage drippings. Scoop out centers of onions and chop fine. Add chopped onions and celery to pan drippings and sauté until celery is limp but not brown. Add to stuffing mix with enough onion water to moisten. Add salt and pepper to taste. Stuff onion shells. Arrange onions in a shallow Pyrex baking dish sprayed with vegetable oil. Pour velouté sauce over onions and sprinkle parsley over top. Bake, unvented, for 10 minutes. Vent in position 1 and bake an additional 35 minutes. When done, onion shells should be fork-tender.

HINTS: Soup purées that make a good sauce for this recipe are Cream of Chicken Soup (p. 50), Cream of Mushroom Soup (p. 60), and Corn and Ham Chowder (p. 54).

4 large onions
½ pound bulk sausage
½ cup diced celery
2 cups Homemade Stuffing Mix (p. 41)
Salt and pepper to taste
1 cup Velouté Sauce I or II (p. 36 and p. 37)
1 tablespoon fresh parsley, chopped

COOK'S NOTES:

Scalloped Summer Squash

SERVES 4–6.

2 small zucchini (about 2 inches in diameter)
2 small yellow squash (about 2 inches in diameter)
1 large onion, sliced very thin
¾ cup coarse cracker crumbs
Salt and pepper to taste
1½ cups Velouté Sauce I or II (p. 36 and p. 37)
1 tablespoon flour
1 tablespoon melted butter

Preheat cast-iron oven to a baking temperature of 375°F. Wash and dry zucchini and summer squash; trim ends and slice into ¼-inch slices. Separate onion slices into rings. Spray an 8½- by 2-inch Pyrex baking dish with vegetable oil. Layer zucchini and summer squash in a circular overlapping pattern, then add a layer of onion rings. Sprinkle with ½ cup of the cracker crumbs and with salt and pepper. Add another layer of squash. Blend velouté sauce with flour and heat until bubbling; pour over squash. Mix remaining ¼ cup of cracker crumbs with melted butter and sprinkle over top of casserole. Bake, vented in position 1, for 45–50 minutes, or until summer squash is fork-tender.

HINTS: Soup purées that make a good substitute for the sauce are Cream of Chicken Soup (p. 50), Cream of Mushroom Soup (p. 60) and Corn and Ham Chowder (p. 54). For a complete meal in a dish, add a layer of thin-sliced cooked ham, chicken, or rabbit.

HINTS: When the vegetable garden gets ahead of you, and soup vegetables such as green beans, yellow beans, peas, zucchini, broccoli, and asparagus go beyond their prime, pick them anyway. Diced, blanched, and frozen, they make great soup vegetables and vegetable purées for soups and sauces. We never seem to have enough asparagus, so as we come to the end of our crop, I deliberately let some grow too large. After cooking the asparagus, I put it through a blender or food processor and then through a food mill, to remove any pieces of tough fiber that remain. This purée makes wonderful garden-fresh-tasting Cream of Fresh Asparagus Soup (p. 58) all winter. All vegetable purées made from vegetables with fibers or strings such as the tough stalks of broccoli, sugar snap peas, string beans, etc., should be put through a food mill or strainer before packaging. Broccoli could be peeled first, but much of the flavor and many nutrients would be lost.

COOK'S NOTES:

Fresh Corn Fritters

18 FRITTERS

Beat egg white until stiff but not dry; set aside. In another bowl beat egg yolk and sugar. Stir in vanilla, milk, cooled corn, rolled oats, and parsley. Add biscuit mix gradually, stirring well to blend. Fold in beaten egg white carefully. Drop by teaspoonfuls into 1½ inches of hot fat in a heavy frying pan. Fry until golden brown, turning just once. Serve with maple syrup.

1 cup fresh or frozen corn, cooked and drained
1 egg, separated
2 tablespoons sugar
1 teaspoon vanilla
2 teaspoons milk
¼ cup quick-cooking rolled oats
1½ teaspoons fresh parsley, chopped very fine
¾ cup Homemade Biscuit Mix (p. 44)
Fat for frying

Scalloped Corn and Tomatoes

SERVES 4.

Preheat cast-iron oven to a baking temperature of 375°F. Partially cook bacon; drain fat and reserve. Spray a 1½-quart Pyrex casserole with vegetable oil. Layer tomatoes, cracker crumbs, and corn, ending with a layer of corn. Mix salt, pepper, reserved fat, and Worcestershire sauce and pour over vegetables. Top with bacon slices and bake, vented in position 1, for 40–50 minutes, or until casserole bubbles in center.

6 slices bacon
4 cups canned tomatoes, drained
1 cup cracker crumbs
2 cups cooked corn, drained
1 teaspoon salt
¼ teaspoon pepper
1 tablespoon Worcestershire sauce (optional)

COOK'S NOTES:

Vermont Baked Squash and Apples

SERVES 4–6.

2 pounds butternut squash,
   peeled, seeded, and cut into
   1-inch cubes
2 large apples, cored and cut into
   wedges
½ cup maple syrup
1 tablespoon cornstarch
¼ cup melted butter
1 teaspoon salt
½ teaspoon cinnamon

Preheat cast-iron oven to a baking temperature of 350°F. Combine squash cubes and apple wedges in a 2-quart casserole dish sprayed with vegetable oil. Stir cornstarch into maple syrup until dissolved, add melted butter and seasonings. Pour over squash. Bake, vented in position 1, for 45–55 minutes.

HINTS: This casserole goes well with ham.

Scalloped Honeyed Tomatoes

SERVES 4.

½ cup chopped onion
¼ cup butter
1 cup coarse dry bread crumbs
4 large tomatoes, blanched,
   peeled, and sliced
Salt and pepper to taste
Fresh or dried sweet basil to taste
Honey
2 tablespoons butter

Preheat cast-iron oven to a baking temperature of 350–375°F. Sauté onion in butter until limp but not brown; stir in bread crumbs. In a 1-quart casserole dish sprayed with vegetable oil, layer tomatoes and bread crumb mixture. Sprinkle each layer lightly with salt and pepper and sweet basil. Drizzle about 1 tablespoon honey on each layer. Dot top of casserole with butter and bake, vented in position 1, for 35–45 minutes.

COOK'S NOTES:

Breads

White Bread

1 LOAF

½ *tablespoon dry yeast*
1¼ *cups warm water*
  (110–115°F)
1 *teaspoon salt*
2 *tablespoons honey*
2 *tablespoons lard or shortening*
2 *tablespoons gluten flour*
3¾ *cups all-purpose unbleached*
  flour

Put yeast, water, salt, honey, lard, gluten flour, and 1 cup of the all-purpose flour in a medium bowl. With an electric mixer or by hand with a wooden spoon, mix well until very smooth. Continue adding all-purpose flour with a mixer or wooden spoon until mixture is too heavy to add any more, then add more flour with a wooden spoon until dough forms a ball that comes away from sides of bowl. Turn out onto a lightly floured board and knead, adding just enough flour to keep dough from sticking to board. Continue kneading until dough is no longer tacky enough to stick to your hands, although it will still feel sticky. It should be reasonably firm. This takes about 8–10 minutes. Place ball of dough in a greased bowl, turning once to grease top of dough. Cover with a heavy towel and let rise until double in bulk. Punch down, knead 5–6 times to get air bubbles out, shape into a round ball, and put in a well-greased round 8-inch casserole or fondue dish, preferably with straight sides. Cover lightly and let rise again until doubled. Meanwhile, preheat cast-iron oven to a baking temperature of 350–375°F. When dough has doubled, quickly slip it into oven and bake, vented in position 2, for 35–40 minutes. Bread will not get very brown on top, but sides and edges around top will brown nicely. When done, bread will be firm around edges, but soft on top. It will not make a hollow sound when tapped, like bread baked in a regular oven. This bread remains fresh for days.

COOK'S NOTES:

Whole-Wheat Bread

1 LOAF

To make whole-wheat bread, substitute 1½ cups whole-wheat flour for 1½ cups of the all-purpose unbleached flour in preceding recipe and follow directions as given for white bread.

Herbed Casserole Bread

1 LOAF

Sprinkle yeast over warm water in a small cup. Warm cottage cheese slightly and put it in a bowl with remaining ingredients except all-purpose flour. Add yeast mixture and beat well. Add all-purpose flour a little at a time, beating well after each addition. Batter should be very stiff. Cover bowl and let dough rise until double. Stir down vigorously with a wooden spoon. Form into a round ball and place in a round Pyrex baking dish sprayed with vegetable oil. Let rise again until double. Meanwhile, preheat cast-iron oven to a baking temperature of 350°F. When batter is doubled, bake, vented in position 2, for about 30 minutes.

HINTS: This bread makes an excellent ham sandwich and is especially good with Italian food.

1 tablespoon dry yeast
3 tablespoons warm water (110–115°F)
½ cup cottage cheese (add 1 tablespoon milk to very dry cheese)
2 tablespoons honey
2 teaspoons dried onion flakes (soak in 1 teaspoon water for 5 minutes)
1½ teaspoons garlic powder
1½ teaspoons dill seed
¾ teaspoon salt
2 teaspoons butter
Pinch baking soda
1 small egg (3 tablespoons), slightly beaten
4 tablespoons gluten flour
1¾ cups all-purpose unbleached flour

COOK'S NOTES:

French Bread

1 cup warm water (110–115°F)
¾ tablespoon dry yeast
1½ teaspoons salt
2 tablespoons gluten flour
2¾ cups all-purpose unbleached flour
Cornmeal

Pour water into a large, tapered bowl. Sprinkle yeast over water and allow to settle for 1–2 minutes. Add salt, gluten flour, and 1 cup of the all-purpose flour. Beat well until smooth. Gradually add remaining all-purpose flour until you have a stiff dough. Use your hands to mix if necessary. Turn dough out onto a floured board or clean counter top and knead for 5–7 minutes until smooth and elastic. Be careful not to overflour your board; put just enough flour down to keep dough from sticking. Let dough rest while you rinse and dry bowl. Put dough back in *ungreased* bowl. Cover with a heavy towel and let rise in a warm place until *tripled* in bulk, about 2 hours. Punch dough down and let rise again until doubled. This second rising takes less than half the time of first. Scrape dough from bowl onto a floured board and shape in 2 oblong rolls that will fit into largest-diameter Pyrex baking dish your oven will hold. Sprinkle cornmeal into baking dish and put in both loaves, with a space of at least 1 inch between loaves. Let dough rise again until double in bulk. *Do not cover this time.* Meanwhile, preheat cast-iron oven to a baking temperature of 375°F. When dough has risen, brush with cold water. Pour ½ inch of hot water into bottom of cast-iron oven and replace cover snugly for 5 minutes. Working quickly, slip baking dish into oven. Vent in position 2 and bake for 25–30 minutes. Move venting to position 3 and bake 10 minutes longer. Brush again with cold water and bake in position 3 for another 15–20 minutes. Remove from baking dish and cool on wire cake racks.

HINTS: Cold water may be combined with a slightly beaten egg white to give a shiny top to your bread.

COOK'S NOTES:

Beaten Batter Rolls

4

16 SMALL ROLLS

Scald milk with honey, lard, and salt. Place mixture in a medium-sized bowl and cool to lukewarm. Add yeast, egg, gluten flour, and ½ cup of the all-purpose flour. Beat well with an electric mixer or by hand until smooth. Gradually add remaining all-purpose flour, incorporating each addition well before going on. Dough should be soft and somewhat sticky, but should hold some form when handling. If it doesn't, add more flour, 1 tablespoon at a time. Place dough in a greased bowl and cover. Let rise until double in bulk, 1–1½ hours. Punch down and shape into sixteen 1-inch balls. Place these balls in an 8½- by 2-inch Pyrex baking dish sprayed with vegetable oil, leaving a space between each roll. Cover again and let rise until double in bulk. Meanwhile, preheat cast-iron oven to a baking temperature of 375°F. When dough is doubled, bake, vented in position 2, for about 17 minutes. Tops will not be browned but will be springy.

6 tablespoons milk
2 tablespoons honey
2 tablespoons lard or shortening
½ teaspoon salt
2 teaspoons dry yeast
1 egg
1 tablespoon gluten flour
1⅔ cups all-purpose unbleached flour

HINTS: This is a very soft dough to work with, so flour your hands well when shaping the rolls. I find it works best to cover my baking dish during the second rising period with something that will not come in contact with the dough. It's so soft that anything like waxed paper or a towel will stick to the tops. A Pyrex casserole cover works well. Lacking one of these, you might try inverting a glass or tin pie plate over the rolls. Then you can cover it with a towel if you want. To reheat leftover rolls, place them in a brown paper bag. Moisten the bag with cold water and place it in a preheated cast-iron oven until the moisture on the bag has evaporated. This takes just about 5 minutes.

COOK'S NOTES:

Coffee Cake

1 COFFEE CAKE

⅓ cup butter
½ cup brown sugar, firmly
  packed
¼ teaspoon cinnamon
⅓ cup chopped nuts
1 recipe Beaten Batter Rolls
  (preceding recipe)

Melt butter in an 8½- by 2-inch Pyrex baking dish. (Make sure sides of baking dish are well buttered too.) Sprinkle brown sugar, cinnamon, and nuts over melted butter. Prepare batter. When it's time to shape rolls, place balls of dough on top of butter and sugar mixture. Preheat cast-iron oven to a baking temperature of 375°F. Proceed with second rising and bake as directed in Beaten Batter Rolls, master recipe. Invert baking dish on a platter and remove rolls as soon as baking dish is removed from oven; otherwise sugar mixture will cool and harden and make it difficult to remove rolls from baking dish.

Orange Tea Rolls

15–16 SMALL ROLLS

1 recipe Beaten Batter Rolls
  (p. 143)
½ cup raisins
¼ cup sugar
1 teaspoon grated orange rind
1 tablespoon orange juice
¼ cup chopped nuts

Follow directions for Beaten Batter Rolls until batter has risen to double in bulk first time. Stir in raisins. Shape rolls and place in an 8½- by 2-inch Pyrex baking dish sprayed with vegetable oil. Mix remaining ingredients and spread over top of rolls. Preheat cast-iron oven to a baking temperature of 375°F. Let rolls rise until double in bulk and bake as directed in Beaten Batter Rolls' master recipe.

COOK'S NOTES:

Popovers

4 X

Popovers are the American version of Yorkshire pudding. The following recipe makes giant popovers that split open by themselves at the top, giving nice crisp edges. Serve them hot from the oven with fresh sweet butter.

Preheat cast-iron oven to a baking temperature of 375°F. Mix egg, salt, and milk with an electric mixer in a small bowl. Add flour with melted butter all at once. Stir until all ingredients are well moistened; *do not overmix.* Divide into four 6-ounce Pyrex baking cups sprayed with vegetable oil and set in a large baking dish. Bake, vented in position 2, for 30 minutes. Carefully move venting to position 3 and bake an additional 10 minutes. *Do not peek or jar the cover during baking.*

1 egg
½ teaspoon salt
½ cup milk
½ cup flour
1 tablespoon melted butter

A Reminder: Even if a recipe calls for a baking temperature of 375°F, you can bake it at lower temperatures, in most instances, just by baking it longer.

COOK'S NOTES:

Baking Powder Drop Biscuits

8 MEDIUM BISCUITS

1 cup all-purpose unbleached
flour
2 teaspoons baking powder
½ teaspoon salt
½ teaspoon cream of tartar
1½ teaspoons sugar
1 tablespoon lard
1 tablespoon butter
½ cup cold milk

Preheat cast-iron oven to a baking temperature of 375°F. Stir flour, baking powder, salt, cream of tartar, and sugar together until thoroughly mixed. Put ½ cup of the mixture in a blender or food processor, or use a bowl with a beater. Add lard, butter, and milk. Blend thoroughly and return to bowl with rest of flour mixture. Mix with a fork until all dry ingredients are incorporated. Drop by large spoonfuls into an 8-inch Pyrex baking dish. Dot each biscuit with a tiny piece of butter. Bake, vented in position 2, for 20 minutes.

HINTS: To make cut biscuits, reduce milk to ⅓ cup.

Quick Drop Biscuits

6 MEDIUM BISCUITS

1 cup Homemade Biscuit Mix
(p. 44)
⅓ cup milk

Preheat cast-iron oven to a baking temperature of 375°F. Add milk to mix. Stir until all mix is moistened. Drop by spoonfuls into a Pyrex pie plate. Shape with a fork for even conformation. Bake, vented in position 2, for 17–18 minutes.

HINTS: If you are using these biscuits for a dessert, add 2 table-spoons sugar. If you are serving them with fricasseed chicken, add ½ teaspoon poultry seasoning or sage.

COOK'S NOTES:

Quick Banana Bread

1 LOAF

Preheat cast-iron oven to a baking temperature of 375°F. Spoon mix into measuring cup; add gluten flour and baking soda; mix well. Blend remaining ingredients, beating until batter is smooth. Add mix and beat well to blend. Pour into a 10- by 3-inch tube pan sprayed with vegetable oil. Bake with paper towels (see Paper Towel Method, p. 22), vented in position 2, for 40–45 minutes, or until a toothpick inserted in center comes out clean. Cool 5 minutes in pan, remove, and finish cooling on a wire cake rack.

HINTS: To make a steamed banana pudding from this recipe, add ¼ cup more of honey and bake without paper towels, vented in position 1, for 1 hour. Serve hot with whipped cream.

2 cups Homemade Biscuit Mix (p. 44)
2 tablespoons gluten flour
¾ teaspoon baking soda
½ cup honey
Scant 1 cup mashed ripe banana
½ cup chopped nuts
2 eggs
⅓ cup sour milk

COOK'S NOTES:

Banana Honey Bread

1 LOAF

1 ¾ cups all-purpose unbleached
  flour
2 tablespoons gluten flour
1 ½ teaspoons baking powder
½ teaspoon baking soda
½ teaspoon salt
¾ cup mashed ripe banana
1 tablespoon lemon juice
½ teaspoon grated lemon rind
  (optional)
6 tablespoons lard or shortening
½ cup honey
1 egg plus 1 egg yolk
6 tablespoons milk
½ cup chopped walnuts

Preheat cast-iron oven to a baking temperature of 375°F. Stir dry ingredients together. Add lemon juice and lemon rind to mashed banana and mix. Cream lard and honey, add eggs and beat thoroughly until very fluffy, about 3 minutes. Add dry ingredients alternately with milk. Stir in banana and nuts. Pour into a 10- by 3-inch tube pan sprayed with vegetable oil and bake with paper towels (see Paper Towel Method, p. 22), vented in position 2, for 50–60 minutes, or until a toothpick inserted in center comes out clean. Cool in pan for 10 minutes, remove, and finish cooling on a wire cake rack.

COOK'S NOTES:

Bran Muffins

6 LARGE MUFFINS

Preheat cast-iron oven to a baking temperature of 375–400°F. Spoon biscuit mix lightly into measuring cup; do not pack. Place egg in a medium bowl. Beat well with a fork, add honey and sour milk. Beat again. Blend in bran, biscuit mix, and baking soda. Stir quickly until all dry ingredients are moistened; batter should not be smooth. Divide into 6 Pyrex baking cups sprayed with vegetable oil. Place cups in a large round baking dish and bake, vented in position 1, for 15 minutes. Move venting to position 2 and bake an additional 15–20 minutes. Muffins will pull away from sides of baking cups a little, but tops will not be very brown. Remove from baking cups immediately.

1 cup Homemade Biscuit Mix
(p. 44)
1 egg
2 tablespoons honey
Scant ½ cup sour milk
⅔ cup whole bran buds
¼ teaspoon baking soda

HINTS: Vary these muffins by substituting ⅓ cup grape-nut flakes for ⅓ cup of bran.

COOK'S NOTES:

Corn Bread

⅓ cup honey

1 egg

½ teaspoon salt

½ cup cornmeal

1 cup all-purpose unbleached
    flour

2 teaspoons baking powder

¼ teaspoon baking soda

1½ teaspoons melted butter

¾ cup milk

Preheat cast-iron oven to a baking temperature of 375°F. Beat honey and egg. Mix salt, cornmeal, flour, baking powder, and baking soda; stir thoroughly. Add dry mixture to honey and egg mixture with melted butter and milk. Beat up quickly, but just until all ingredients are moistened. Place in an 8½- by 2-inch Pyrex baking dish sprayed with vegetable oil. Bake with paper towels (see Paper Towel Method, p. 22), vented in position 1, for 15 minutes. Remove paper towels and bake an additional 5–7 minutes, or until a toothpick inserted in center comes out clean.

COOK'S NOTES:

Desserts

Cheesecake

ONE 9-INCH CHEESECAKE

2 eggs plus 1 egg yolk
8 ounces softened cream cheese
½ cup sugar
⅛ teaspoon salt
1 teaspoon vanilla
2½ teaspoons lemon juice
1½ cups sour cream
Graham Cracker Crust for
9-inch crust (p. 45)

Preheat cast-iron oven to a baking temperature of 350°F. Beat eggs and egg yolk until light and lemon colored. Add remaining ingredients except sour cream and crust and blend until smooth. Add sour cream and blend until well incorporated. Pour into prepared graham cracker crust. Bake, vented in position 2, for 30–35 minutes. Cheesecake is done when a slight crack appears in custard near edge; center will still appear soft. A knife inserted in center *will not* come out clean.) Cool and chill several hours before serving.

HINTS: This cheesecake is delicious served with homemade strawberry, raspberry, or apricot preserves.

COOK'S NOTES:

Angel Food Cake

1 SMALL ROUND LOAF CAKE

Preheat cast-iron oven to a baking temperature of 375°F. Sift flour twice with ¼ cup of the sugar; set aside. Beat egg whites with remaining ingredients until they are stiff enough to form soft peaks, but are still moist and glossy. Add remaining ½ cup sugar, 2 tablespoons at a time, until egg whites hold stiff peaks. Sift one-third of the flour mixture over whites and fold in carefully; repeat until flour is used up. Turn into an ungreased 1-quart round Pyrex casserole dish. Bake with paper towels (see Paper Towel Method, p. 22), vented in position 2, for 40–50 minutes. When cake is done, it should spring back when pressed with your finger, and top should not be sticky. Remove baking dish from oven and cool cake in dish, *upside down.* You may have to use something to support dish in order to do this. When cake is cold, remove from baking dish.

½ cup sifted all-purpose
    unbleached flour
¾ cup sugar
¾ cup egg whites
½ teaspoon cream of tartar
Dash salt
1 teaspoon vanilla
¼ teaspoon almond extract

HINTS: Late winter afternoons or early evenings, when days grow cooler and more heat is called for, are the best times to bake cakes and breads that require high baking temperatures.

COOK'S NOTES:

Pound Cake

1 SMALL CAKE

¾ cup butter
½ teaspoon grated lemon rind
¾ cup sugar
1 teaspoon vanilla
3 eggs
1¼ cups all-purpose unbleached
   flour
½ teaspoon baking soda
¼ teaspoon salt

Preheat cast-iron oven to a baking temperature of 375°F. Cream butter with lemon rind, then gradually add sugar and cream until light and very fluffy, blending at least 3 minutes on medium speed with an electric mixer. Add vanilla, then eggs, one at a time. Beat well after each addition. Mix dry ingredients thoroughly and stir in. Grease *bottom only* of an 8½- by 2-inch Pyrex baking dish and pour batter into dish. Bake with paper towels (see Paper Towel Method, p. 22), vented in position 2, for 25–30 minutes. Cool in pan.

HINTS: To make a pretty pattern on the top of the cake, take a paper doily and place it over the cake, then sift confectioner's sugar over the top. Remove the doily.

COOK'S NOTES:

Applesauce Seed Cake

SERVES 10.

Preheat cast-iron oven to a baking temperature of 375°F. Cream honey and lard. Add egg, beating well. Sift dry ingredients and add alternately with applesauce to honey mixture. Mix well, then add raisins and sunflower seeds. Pour into a 10- by 3-inch tube pan sprayed with vegetable oil. Bake with paper towels (see Paper Towel Method, p. 22), vented in position 2, for 50–60 minutes, or until a toothpick inserted in center comes out clean.

HINTS: This cake can be served plain or with Honey Egg Frosting (p. 162).

⅔ cup honey or ¾ cup sugar
¼ cup lard or shortening
1 egg
1⅓ cups all-purpose unbleached flour
3 tablespoons gluten flour
¾ teaspoon salt
1 teaspoon cinnamon
¾ teaspoon cloves
½ teaspoon nutmeg
1 teaspoon baking soda
1 cup unsweetened applesauce
¼ cup raisins
½ cup sunflower seeds or chopped nuts

COOK'S NOTES:

Dried-Fruit Cake

SERVES 16.

1½ cups good quality mixed
  dried fruits (apples, prunes,
  pears, apricots, honey-dipped
  pineapple, etc.)
¾ cup port wine
2 eggs, separated
¾ cup butter
¾ cup honey
1½ cups all-purpose unbleached
  flour
½ cup whole-wheat flour
1 teaspoon baking soda
½ teaspoon salt
1 teaspoon cinnamon
½ teaspoon nutmeg
¼ teaspoon cloves
½ cup light raisins
½ cup dark raisins
1 cup chopped dates
1 tablespoon grated orange rind
¾ cup chopped mixed nuts

Soak dried fruit in port wine to cover overnight. In morning, drain fruit well (for at least 1 hour), reserving wine. Preheat cast-iron oven to a baking temperature of 350°F. When the fruit has drained, beat egg whites until stiff but not dry; set aside. Cream butter and honey; add egg yolks and beat well. Mix all-purpose and whole-wheat flours, soda, salt, and spices; stir with a fork to mix thoroughly. Add flour mixture alternately with ¾ cup of wine drained from fruit to the butter, honey, and egg yolk mixture. Fold in drained fruits, raisins, dates, orange rind, and nuts. Carefully fold in egg whites until none of white is visible. Turn into a 10- by 3-inch tube pan sprayed with vegetable oil. Push batter up toward sides of pan so cake will rise evenly. Bake with paper towels (see Paper Towel Method, p. 22), vented in position 2, for 55–60 minutes, or until a toothpick inserted in center comes out clean. Once cake is in oven, it is safe to allow temperature to fall back to 325°F. Cool cake in pan for 5 minutes, remove from pan, and cool on a cake rack. After cake has cooled, wrap well in foil and store in a cool place at least 2 weeks before eating. As with all fruitcakes, the longer the cake ripens, the better it will be. Slice thin to serve.

HINTS: For added flavor and a real holiday touch, wrap cooled cake in a rum-soaked piece of muslin before storing in foil. Re-soak the muslin every week or so for a few weeks—if the cake lasts that long!

COOK'S NOTES:

Honey Date Cake

SERVES 8.

Preheat cast-iron oven to a baking temperature of 375°F. Combine dates and boiling water. Cool to room temperature. Cream lard and honey until light and fluffy. Add vanilla and egg; beat well. Mix dry ingredients thoroughly and add to creamed mixture alternately with date mix. Stir in nuts. Pour batter into an 8-inch round Pyrex cake dish sprayed with vegetable oil. Bake with paper towels (see Paper Towel Method, p. 22), vented in position 2, for 20 minutes. Remove paper towels and bake in position 2 an additional 5–8 minutes. Cool for 5 minutes in pan. Finish cooling on a cake rack.

HINTS: If you use dates that are already chopped and sugar coated, pack them well in order to get the proper amount for the recipe. In this recipe, I reduce the boiling water to ¼ cup when using this type of date.

¾ cup pitted dates, chopped small
½ cup boiling water
¼ cup lard or shortening
6 tablespoons honey
½ teaspoon vanilla
1 egg
¾ cup sifted all-purpose unbleached flour
1 tablespoon gluten flour
½ teaspoon baking soda
⅛ teaspoon salt
⅓ cup chopped nuts

COOK'S NOTES:

Chocolate Fudge Cake

SERVES 8.

1 egg, separated
½ cup dry baking cocoa or carob powder
1½ cups all-purpose unbleached flour
1½ teaspoons salt
1¼ teaspoons baking powder
1 teaspoon baking soda
Scant ½ cup salad oil
¾ cup honey
1 teaspoon vanilla
½ cup milk
½ cup boiling water

Preheat cast-iron oven to a baking temperature of 375°F. Beat egg white until stiff but not dry. Place egg yolk in a medium-sized bowl with remaining ingredients *except* boiling water. Beat until well blended and smooth. Add boiling water and blend thoroughly. Fold in egg whites until all white disappears. Pour into a 10- by 3-inch tube pan sprayed with vegetable oil. Bake with paper towels (see Paper Towel Method, p. 22), vented in position 2, for 35–40 minutes, or until a toothpick inserted in center comes out clean.

HINTS: Frost with Chocolate Mallow Frosting (p. 163).

Gingerbread

SERVES 8.

1¼ cups all-purpose unbleached flour
1 teaspoon baking soda
½ teaspoon cloves
¼ teaspoon powdered ginger
½ teaspoon cinnamon
½ teaspoon salt
¼ cup honey
¼ cup lard or shortening
½ cup molasses
½ cup sour milk
1 egg

Preheat cast-iron oven to a baking temperature of 375°F. Stir dry ingredients together until well mixed. Add honey, lard, molasses, and milk. Beat 1½ minutes on low speed with an electric mixer. Scrape sides of bowl and beaters, add egg, and beat another 1½ minutes on low speed. Pour into an 8½- by 2-inch Pyrex baking dish sprayed with vegetable oil. Bake with paper towels (see Paper Towel Method, p. 22), vented in position 2, for 25–35 minutes, or until a toothpick inserted in center comes out clean. Serve warm with whipped cream.

COOK'S NOTES:

White Cake

Preheat cast-iron oven to a baking temperature of 375°F. Beat egg white until stiff but not dry; set aside. Cream lard and honey in a medium-sized bowl until mixture is light and fluffy. Stir dry ingredients together until thoroughly mixed; add to lard mixture. Add egg yolk and ¼ cup of the milk. Mix until flour is moistened. Beat 2 minutes on medium speed with an electric mixer or 500 strokes by hand. Add remaining milk and vanilla and beat 2 minutes longer. Fold in egg white until no more white is visible. Pour into an 8½- by 2-inch Pyrex baking dish sprayed with vegetable oil. Bake with paper towels (see Paper Towel Method, p. 22), vented in position 2, for 30–35 minutes, or until a toothpick inserted in center comes out clean. Cool 5 minutes in baking dish; finish cooling on cake rack.

1 egg, separated
4 tablespoons lard or shortening
Scant ½ cup honey
1½ teaspoons baking powder
⅛ teaspoon baking soda
¼ teaspoon salt
1 cup all-purpose unbleached flour
Scant ½ cup milk
1 teaspoon vanilla

HINTS: **This recipe makes a thick single layer; doubled, it would make a large layer cake for special occasions.**

COOK'S NOTES:

Pineapple Upside-Down Cake

SERVES 6–8.

¼ cup lard or shortening
¼ teaspoon salt
½ teaspoon vanilla
6 tablespoons honey
1 egg
1 cup all-purpose unbleached
    flour
1½ teaspoons baking powder
⅛ teaspoon baking soda
6 tablespoons milk
¼ cup butter
½ cup firmly packed brown
    sugar
1-pound can sliced pineapple

Preheat cast-iron oven to a baking temperature of 375°F. Cream lard, salt, vanilla, and honey until light and fluffy. Add egg and beat thoroughly. Stir flour, baking powder, and baking soda together until well mixed. Add flour mixture to batter alternately with milk, beating well after each addition. Melt butter and stir sugar into it. Pour into an 8½- by 2-inch Pyrex baking dish sprayed with vegetable oil. Arrange pineapple slices in dish over sugar mixture. Pour cake batter over top. Bake with paper towels (see Paper Towel Method, p. 22), vented in position 2, for 35 minutes, or until a toothpick inserted in center comes out clean. Loosen cake from sides of pan and invert immediately onto a serving platter, removing baking dish. Serve warm or cold with whipped cream.

COOK'S NOTES:

Fresh Raspberry Teacake

SERVES 8.

Preheat cast-iron oven to a baking temperature of 375°F. Beat honey with egg. Mix salt, flour, and baking powder thoroughly. Add to egg mixture with milk all at once. Stir up quickly until all ingredients are barely moistened. Stir in melted butter and raspberries. Pour batter into an 8½- by 2-inch Pyrex baking dish sprayed with vegetable oil. Bake with paper towels (see Paper Towel Method, p. 22), vented in position 2, for 25–30 minutes, or until a toothpick inserted in center comes out clean.

HINTS: The fresh, tart flavor of raspberries gives this teacake an unusual flavor; more honey may be used if it is too tart for you. Blueberries or blackberries may be substituted for the raspberries.

⅓ cup honey

1 egg

½ teaspoon salt

1½ cups all-purpose unbleached flour

2 teaspoons baking powder

¾ cup milk

1½ teaspoons melted butter

½ cup cleaned raspberries (picked over but not rinsed)

COOK'S NOTES:

Honey Egg Frosting

FROSTS CENTER AND TOP OF A TWO-LAYER CAKE OR TOP AND SIDES OF A ONE-LAYER CAKE.

⅛ teaspoon cream of tartar
1 teaspoon cornstarch
Dash salt
1 egg white, at room
   temperature
½ cup honey
½ teaspoon vanilla

Mix cream of tartar, cornstarch, and salt together in a small cup. Sift cornstarch mixture through a tea strainer over egg white in a medium bowl with a narrow bottom. Beat mixture just until egg white is slightly frothy. Heat honey in a small pan until it is too hot to touch. Add honey to egg mixture in a slow stream, beating constantly. Add vanilla and continue to beat mixture until it forms firm peaks that hold up when beater is taken out.

HINTS: This is especially good with Applesauce Seed Cake (p. 155).

COOK'S NOTES:

Chocolate Mallow Frosting

FROSTS A DOUBLE-LAYER CAKE.

Place all ingredients except vanilla in a heavy 1-quart saucepan and cook over low heat on an iron trivet or in a double boiler, stirring constantly, until chocolate and marshmallows are melted and mixture is very thick. Add vanilla and cool, stirring often.

HINTS: You may leave the marshmallows out of the frosting, but if you do, omit the water.

13–14 ounces sweetened condensed milk
2 ounces unsweetened chocolate
1 cup miniature marshmallows
2 tablespoons water
Dash salt
½ teaspoon vanilla

Chocolate Sauce

For a delicious ice cream sauce, thin Chocolate Mallow Frosting with boiling water to desired consistency and use pure rum extract instead of vanilla.

COOK'S NOTES:

Carob Chip Cookies

2 DOZEN SMALL COOKIES

1 ½ cups Homemade Biscuit Mix
   (p. 44)
½ cup granulated sugar
¼ cup firmly packed brown
   sugar
1 well beaten egg
1 teaspoon vanilla
2 teaspoons hot water
½ cup chopped butternuts
1 cup carob chips

Preheat cast-iron oven to a baking temperature of 375°F. Stir biscuit mix and sugars together. Add egg, vanilla, and hot water. Blend thoroughly. Stir in nuts and carob chips. Divide mixture into two 9-inch Pyrex pie plates sprayed with vegetable oil and pat thin. Bake, 1 pie plate at a time, vented in position 3, for 17–18 minutes. Edges will be slightly brown, but not tops. Remove from oven, cut into small "bar cookies," and let set until partially cooled, about 20 minutes. Remove cookies from pie plates and finish cooling on cake racks.

HINTS: Walnuts and chocolate chips may be substituted for the butternuts and carob chips. Carob chips may be purchased from food cooperatives and natural food stores.

COOK'S NOTES:

Sugar Cookies

2 DOZEN SMALL COOKIES

Preheat cast-iron oven to a baking temperature of 375°F. Stir biscuit mix, sugar, and spices together. Add milk, egg, and vanilla and mix well. Stir in raisins. Divide mixture into two 9-inch Pyrex pie plates sprayed with vegetable oil and pat thin. Bake, vented in position 3, 1 pie plate at a time, for 17–18 minutes. Edges will be brown, but not tops. Remove from oven, cut into small "bar cookies," and let set until partially cooled, about 20 minutes. Remove cookies from pie plates and finish cooling on cake racks.

1 ½ cups Homemade Biscuit Mix (p. 44)
½ cup brown sugar
⅛ teaspoon cinnamon
⅛ teaspoon allspice
⅛ teaspoon cloves
2 tablespoons milk
1 slightly beaten egg
½ teaspoon vanilla
½ cup raisins

Honey Brownies

20 BROWNIES

Preheat cast-iron oven to a baking temperature of 375°F. Melt chocolate over hot water; cool. Mix dry ingredients together. Beat eggs till light; add honey, oil, and chocolate; blend well. Add flour mixture, vanilla, and nuts and blend well again. Pour into a 10-inch Pyrex pie plate sprayed with vegetable oil. Bake, vented in position 2, for 25–35 minutes, or until a toothpick inserted in center comes out clean.

HINTS: This recipe baked in the 10-inch pie plate makes a thick cake-type brownie. If you would like a thinner brownie, divide the batter into two 8-inch pie plates and reduce the baking time.

2 ounces unsweetened chocolate
¾ cup all-purpose unbleached flour
½ teaspoon baking powder
¼ teaspoon baking soda
¾ teaspoon salt
2 eggs
¾ cup honey
½ cup salad oil
1 teaspoon vanilla
½ cup chopped nuts

COOK'S NOTES:

Doughnut Babies

2 cups lard for frying
2 eggs, separated
⅓ cup sugar
¼ teaspoon mace
¼ teaspoon cinnamon
¼ teaspoon nutmeg
¼ cup milk
¼ cup quick-cooking oats
1 ½ cups Homemade Biscuit Mix
(p. 44)

While preparing batter, slowly heat lard to 375°F in a cast-iron Dutch oven or a heavy, deep-sided saucepan. Beat egg whites until stiff; set aside. In another bowl, beat egg yolks; add sugar, spices, milk, and rolled oats. Add biscuit mix gradually. Stir to blend thoroughly. Carefully fold in egg whites. Drop by heaping teaspoonfuls into hot lard and fry until golden brown on both sides. Drain on paper towels. May be rolled in granulated sugar seasoned with cinnamon.

HINTS: Be sure not to make these doughnuts too large, or they will brown too much on the outside before they have a chance to cook on the inside.

COOK'S NOTES:

Apple Pie

ONE 9-INCH PIE

Preheat cast-iron oven to a baking temperature of 375°F. Line a 9-inch Pyrex pie plate with crust. Arrange apples on top of crust. Mix 1 cup of the sugar with flour and spices. Pour over apples, shaking pie plate so sugar will go down into apple slices. Drizzle lemon juice over apples and dot with butter. Top with crust. Glaze according to piecrust tips, page 43, and top with remaining 1 tablespoon sugar. Cut steam vents. Bake, vented in position 1, for 45–60 minutes. Baking time will depend greatly on type of apples you use. Move venting to position 2 and bake an additional 15 minutes.

Rich Piecrust dough for 9-inch double-crust pie (p. 45)
6 cups tart apples, pared, cored, and sliced
¾ cup plus 1 tablespoon sugar
2 tablespoons flour
¾ teaspoon cinnamon or nutmeg (I like a little of each)
⅛ teaspoon salt
1 teaspoon lemon juice
1 tablespoon butter

HINTS: I do not like to cook my apple pies so much that the apples are mushy. Apples should be tender, but should hold their shape. If you like a mushy apple, cook the pie a little longer. Maple syrup may be substituted for the sugar in this recipe. If you do so, use 1 cup syrup and add 1 tablespoon cornstarch to the flour and spices before mixing them with the syrup.

COOK'S NOTES:

Berry Pie

ONE 8-INCH PIE

Rich Piecrust dough for 8-inch double-crust pie (p. 45)
3 cups fresh or frozen berries (blackberries, raspberries or cherries)
1 cup plus 1 tablespoon sugar
2½ tablespoons quick-cooking tapioca
1 tablespoon lemon juice
1 tablespoon butter

Preheat cast-iron oven to a baking temperature of 375°F. Fit bottom crust into an 8-inch Pyrex pie plate. Cover with berries. Mix sugar and tapioca and add to berries, distributing evenly. Drizzle lemon juice over mixture and dot with butter. Top with crust, seal and flute edges (see piecrust tips, p. 43). Sprinkle top crust with remaining tablespoon of sugar. Cut steam vents. Bake, vented in position 1, for 45 minutes. Move venting to position 2 and bake 20 minutes longer. Cool on cake rack.

HINTS: If you use frozen berries, you should defrost them in a bowl, mix the tapioca with the berry juices, and let it stand at least 15 minutes before adding it to the crust. This softens the tapioca and will help to prevent a soggy bottom crust.

Blueberry Pie

ONE 9-INCH PIE

Rich Piecrust dough for 9-inch double-crust pie (p. 45)
2 cups blueberries, cleaned and rinsed
1 cup plus 1 tablespoon sugar
2½ tablespoons quick-cooking tapioca
1½ tablespoons lemon juice (1 tablespoon for wild blueberries)
1 tablespoon butter

Preheat cast-iron oven to a baking temperature of 375°F. Line a 9-inch Pyrex pie plate with crust. Add blueberries. Mix 1 cup of the sugar and tapioca; pour over berries. Drizzle lemon juice over berries and dot with butter. Add top crust (see piecrust tips, p. 43). Sprinkle top crust with remaining tablespoon of sugar. Cut steam vents. Bake, vented in position 1, for 45 minutes. Move venting to position 2 and bake an additional 20–35 minutes.

HINTS: If you substitute frozen blueberries for fresh, use 2½ cups berries. This pie is especially pretty with a lattice-type crust.

COOK'S NOTES:

Lemon Meringue Pie

I've tried many lemon meringue pies in the 28 years I've been cooking, but this recipe I copied from my mother's file remains my favorite.

Bake crust according to recipe directions. Cool.

Piecrust
Quick and Easy Piecrust dough
for 9-inch single-crust pie
(p. 44)

Preheat cast-iron oven to a baking temperature of 375–400°F. Mix sugar, cornstarch, flour, and salt in a heavy 2-quart saucepan. Slowly add hot water, stirring constantly. Cook mixture until it comes to a boil, then cook 2 minutes longer. Remove pan from stove and stir small amount of mixture into egg yolks. Return to saucepan, bring to a boil, and cook for 2 minutes, stirring constantly, until thickened. Add butter, lemon rind, and lemon juice. Stir well. Cool 5 minutes, stirring twice. Pour into baked pastry shell and top with meringue.

Filling
1 ¼ cups sugar
3 tablespoons cornstarch
3 tablespoons all-purpose flour
⅛ teaspoon salt
1 ½ cups hot water
3 slightly beaten egg yolks
2 tablespoons butter
1 teaspoon grated lemon rind
⅓ cup fresh lemon juice

Beat egg whites and vanilla until slightly foamy. Add cream of tartar and continue beating, slowly adding sugar until mixture holds stiff peaks when beater is removed. Stir in grated lemon rind. Spread meringue on top of filling, making sure to go to edge of crust: otherwise meringue will shrink and pull away from sides of pie when baking. Bake, vented in position 3, for 16 minutes. Remove from oven, cool, and refrigerate at least 2 hours before serving.

Meringue
3 egg whites
½ teaspoon vanilla
¼ teaspoon cream of tartar
6 tablespoons sugar
½ teaspoon grated lemon rind

COOK'S NOTES:

Coconut Custard Pie

ONE 9-INCH PIE

4 slightly beaten eggs
½ cup sugar
½ teaspoon salt
2 cups milk
1 teaspoon vanilla
½ teaspoon coconut extract
¾ cup shredded coconut
Quick and Easy Piecrust dough
   for 9-inch single-crust pie
   (p. 44)

Preheat cast-iron oven to a baking temperature of 375°F. Mix all ingredients for filling. Working quickly, place *unfilled* piecrust in oven, then pour filling into crust. Bake, vented in position 1, for 40–45 minutes, or until a knife inserted 1½ inches from center comes out clean.

HINTS: See piecrust tips, page 43. To make a plain custard pie, omit coconut and coconut extract and sprinkle the top of the unbaked custard with ¼ teaspoon nutmeg. Custard pies seem to set very rapidly in a cast-iron oven, so watch them carefully so as not to overbake.

Pumpkin Pie

ONE 9-INCH PIE

2 cups pumpkin
1 tablespoon cornstarch
1 teaspoon cinnamon
¼ teaspoon ginger
½ teaspoon nutmeg
Scant ½ teaspoon salt
1½ tablespoons melted butter
1 cup milk
½ cup cream
1 cup brown sugar
2 eggs
Piecrust dough for 9-inch
   single-crust pie (p. 44)

Preheat cast-iron oven to a baking temperature of 375°F. Mix all ingredients for filling in a blender or food processor until smooth. Working quickly, place *unfilled* piecrust in oven, then pour filling into crust. Bake, vented in position 1, for 35–40 minutes, or until a knife inserted 1½ inches from center comes out clean. Serve warm or cold with whipped cream.

HINTS: See piecrust tips, page 43. Custard pies seem to set very rapidly in a cast-iron oven, so watch them carefully so as not to overbake.

COOK'S NOTES:

Mom's Apple Pudding

SERVES 6.

Preheat cast-iron oven to a baking temperature of 375°F. Cut apples into thin slices. Lay in an 8½- by 2-inch round Pyrex baking dish sprayed with vegetable oil. Sprinkle with spices and a little of the sugar. Cream butter and the rest of the sugar with egg until well blended. Stir baking powder into flour until thoroughly mixed. Add dry ingredients alternately with milk to creamed mixture. Beat thoroughly. Pour over apples. Bake with paper towels (see Paper Towel Method, p. 22), vented in position 2, for 30–40 minutes, or until a toothpick inserted in center of cake mixture comes out dry. Serve warm.

3 very large apples, peeled and cored
¼ teaspoon nutmeg
½ teaspoon cinnamon
1 cup sugar
1 tablespoon butter
1 egg
1 teaspoon baking powder
1¼ cups all-purpose unbleached flour
½ cup milk

HINTS: This is usually served with whipped cream, but it's extra delicious with vanilla ice cream.

COOK'S NOTES:

Baked Chocolate Float

SERVES 6–8.

1½ cups sugar
1 cup water
2 tablespoons butter
1 teaspoon vanilla
1 cup all-purpose unbleached
  flour
4 tablespoons unsweetened cocoa
1 teaspoon baking powder
½ teaspoon salt
½ cup milk
½ cup chopped nuts

Preheat cast-iron oven to a baking temperature of 375°F. Combine 1 cup of the sugar with water in a heavy 1-quart saucepan. Boil 5 minutes; set aside. Cream butter and remaining ½ cup of sugar; add vanilla. Mix dry ingredients and add to butter mixture alternately with milk; beat thoroughly. Stir in nuts. Pour hot syrup into a 2-quart Pyrex baking dish sprayed with vegetable oil and drop batter by the spoonful over syrup. Bake, vented in position 2, for 25–30 minutes. Serve hot or cold with whipped cream.

Mom's Date Pudding

SERVES 6.

1 cup boiling water
1 cup granulated sugar
1 tablespoon butter
½ cup brown sugar
1 cup all-purpose unbleached
  flour
1 tablespoon baking powder
½ cup milk
½ cup chopped dates
½ cup chopped nuts

Preheat cast-iron oven to a baking temperature of 375°F. Put boiling water and granulated sugar in a small saucepan. Let boil 5 minutes; set aside. Cream butter and brown sugar together. Mix flour and baking powder thoroughly. Alternately add flour mixture and milk to brown sugar mixture, beating well after each addition. Stir in dates and nuts. Pour hot syrup into a 2-quart Pyrex casserole dish sprayed with vegetable oil. Pour batter in center and spread it slightly; it will spread itself more when it starts to bake. Bake, vented in position 2, for 25–30 minutes. Serve warm or cold with whipped cream or vanilla ice cream.

COOK'S NOTES:

Fruit Crisp

SERVES 6.

Put all ingredients in a large, deep bowl and combine with an electric mixer or your hands until mixture resembles coarse meal. Store in a tightly covered container in refrigerator.

Topping
Makes enough topping for several fruit crisps. (About 5½ cups.)
1 cup butter
1⅓ cups firmly packed brown sugar
1½ cups all-purpose unbleached flour
1½ cups rolled oats
1½ teaspoons nutmeg
3 teaspoons cinnamon
3 tablespoons granulated sugar
½ cup toasted wheat germ

Preheat cast-iron oven to a baking temperature of 350°F. Butter a round Pyrex baking dish *very* generously; sprinkle brown sugar on bottom of dish and cover with fruit. Top with enough fruit-crisp topping to cover fruit completely about ¼ inch thick. Bake, vented in position 1, for 30 minutes; move venting to position 2 and bake an additional 30 minutes. Serve with ice cream or fresh whipped cream.

Fruit
Butter
½ cup brown sugar
3 cups raw fruit, sliced or canned fruit, drained and sliced

HINTS: You can reduce the last half of the baking time by 15 minutes if you remember to bring the fruit-crisp topping to room temperature before baking.

COOK'S NOTES:

Steamed Thanksgiving Pudding

SERVES 16.

¾ cup all-purpose unbleached
  flour
¼ cup whole-wheat flour
1 teaspoon baking soda
1 teaspoon salt
1 teaspoon cinnamon
¾ teaspoon mace
¼ teaspoon nutmeg
2 cups cut raisins
1 cup currants
2 cups mixed honey-dipped
  fruits, cut small
½ cup chopped walnuts
1½ cups soft bread crumbs
½ pound ground suet (about 2
  cups lightly packed)
1 cup packed brown sugar
3 beaten eggs
⅓ cup grape or wine jelly
¼ cup orange juice

Spray a 10- by 3-inch tube cake tin with vegetable oil. Measure flours, soda, salt, and spices into a large bowl. Stir in fruits, nuts and bread crumbs. Mix suet, brown sugar, eggs, jelly, and orange juice; stir into flour mixture. Pour into cake tin and cover with aluminum foil. Place tin on rack in cast-iron Dutch oven, and pour boiling water just to top of rack. *Do not bring water up around cake tin.* Keep water simmering over low-to-medium heat and steam pudding for 4 hours, or until a toothpick inserted in center comes out clean. If it becomes necessary to add more water, do it quickly, removing cover as little as necessary. When done, unmold and slice. Serve warm with hard sauce.

COOK'S NOTES:

Rice Pudding

SERVES 4.

Preheat cast-iron oven to a baking temperature of 275°F. Combine all ingredients in an 8½- by 2-inch Pyrex baking dish sprayed with vegetable oil. Bake, vented in position 1, for 2–3 hours, until rice has absorbed all the milk. Stir occasionally.

½ cup uncooked rice, rinsed in cold water and drained
4 cups milk
1 tablespoon butter
¼ cup honey
½ teaspoon salt
⅛ teaspoon nutmeg
½ cup raisins

HINTS: This is a good recipe for a warmer day when your heater is not going full blast. It can be cooked at even lower temperatures for longer periods of time. If you would like to make this on a colder day and feel that your stove is too hot, place a heavy metal trivet under your cast-iron oven to raise it up from the heat. For the raisins you may substitute chopped dates, prunes, or apricots that have been soaked in water.

COOK'S NOTES:

INDEX

a

adapting recipes for stovetop baking, 20, 25
  for fruit bread (hint), 140
  venting for, 12, 14
agateware roaster, *see* roaster
angel food cake, 153
apple(s):
  baked with butternut squash, 138
  pie, 167
  pudding, 171
applesauce seed cake, 155
asparagus soup, cream of, 58

b

baked beans, 128
baking dishes for stovetop cooking, 10-11
  size of, 26, 27
baking methods, 4-5, 14
  browning casserole tops, 21
  paper towel method, 22-3 and *illus.*
  preheating, 16, 18, 23
  trouble-shooting, 26-7
  see also Dutch oven
baking powder biscuits, 146
banana:
  bread, 147, 148
  pudding, 147
beans, dry:
  baked, 128
  buying, 128
  see also lentils
beans, green, in casserole, 133
beef, 64-78
  baked stuffed, 79
  and biscuits, topsy-turvy, 75
  boiled dinner, 72
  and broccoli, stir-fried, 74
  in Burgundy sauce, 66
  corned, *see* corned beef
  ground, *see* hamburg
  and noodles, spicy, 69
  pepper steak, 77
  pot roast, 68
  roast: prime rib, 64; with Yorkshire pudding, 65 and
    illus.
  spareribs, *see* spareribs: beef
  stew, 51, 66, 67
  stock, 32
  Swiss steak, 70
  see also corned beef; hamburg
berry pie, 168
biscuits:
  baking powder, 146
  and beef, topsy-turvy, 75
  mix, 44

  quick drop type, 146
blackberry:
  pie, 168
  teacake, 161
blueberry:
  pie, 168
  teacake, 161
boiled dinner, 72
  soup, 52
bran muffins, 149
breads, 140-50
  baking temperatures for, 7, 25-6
  banana, 147, 148
  coffee cake, 144
  corn, 150
  French, 142
  herbed, 141
  paper-towel method of baking, 22-3 and *illus.*
  rising, 26
  white, 140
  whole-wheat, 141
  see also biscuits; muffins; rolls
bricks:
  as food-warmers, 20
  as trivets, 7 and *illus.*
broccoli:
  and beef, stir-fried, 74
  -cheese soup, 58
  with Sunday supper chicken, 96
brownies, honey, 165
browning tops of casseroles, 20
buttered crumb topping, 40
butternut squash, baked with apples, 138

c

cabbage:
  casserole, 134
  soup, 52
cake rack, *see* rack (metal)
cakes, 152-61
  angel food, 153
  applesauce seed, 155
  baking temperature for, 7, 25-6
  cheesecake, 152
  chocolate fudge, 158
  falling (hints for remedying), 26
  fruit, 156
  gingerbread, 158
  honey date, 157
  paper towel method of baking, 22-3 and *illus.*
  pineapple upside-down, 160
  pound, 154
  raspberry teacake, 161
  white, 159
carob chip cookies, 164
cast-iron Dutch oven, *see* Dutch oven

cauliflower-shrimp supreme, 107
celery soup, cream of, 58
Celsius/Fahrenheit temperatures, 23, *table* 27
charcoal grilling, 4-5
  heat control, 7
cheese:
  -broccoli soup, 58
  and macaroni, 120, 121
  omelet, 124
  and onion strata, 125
  -tomato soup, 61
cheesecake, 152
cherry pie, 168
chicken:
  casserole, quick and easy, 96
  fried, 102
  fruited, 92
  honey soy, 90
  meat thermometer, placement in, *illus.* 95
  with scalloped squash, 136
  soup, 50
  -spaghetti bake, 91
  stack-up dinner, 89
  stock, 33
  and sugar snap peas, stir-fried, 88
  for Sunday supper, 96
  Verona style, 92
  in wine sauce, 100
  see also recipes for rabbit
chili, 78
Chinese dishes:
  egg rolls, 126 and *illus.*
  fried rice, 127
  turkey chow mein, 97
  see also stir-fried meals
chocolate:
  float, baked, 172
  fudge cake, 158
  honey brownies, 165
  mallow frosting, 163
  sauce, 163
chowder, *see* soups
clam(s):
  in fish sauce, 37
  -onion quiche, 109
  scalloped: with corn, 106; with mushrooms, 106
coal stove, 3, 6
  quick hot fire in, 7
  refueling, 6, 8
  regulation of surface temperature, *illus.* 7, 8
coconut custard pie, 170
coffee cake, 144
cookies:
  carob chip, 164
  honey brownies, 165
  sugar, 165
corn:
  bread, 150
  fritters, 137
  and ham chowder, 54
  scalloped: with clams, 106; with sausage, 85; with
    tomatoes, 137
  in shepherd's pie, 74
corned beef:
  boiled dinner, 72

hash, 76
crab:
  bisque, 48
  Newburg, 111
  in seafood casserole, 108
cream puffs, 46
crepes, poultry filling for, 100
Crock-Pot, 4, 25
  for keeping foods warm, 20
crumb topping, buttered, 40

d

date:
  -honey cake, 157
  pudding, 172
desserts, 152-75
  cakes, 152-61
  cookies, 164-5
  frostings, 162-3
  pies, 167-70
  puddings, 171-5
dishes for baking in stove-top oven, 10-11
  size of, 26, 27
doughnut babies, 166
dressing, *see* stuffing
duckling à l'orange, 93
Dutch oven, 4-5, *illus.* 11
  cover, lined with foil, 5, 11 and *illus.*
  preheating, 16, 18, 23
  preparation for baking, 11 and *illus., illus.* 26
  seasoning of, 11
  selection of, 9
  size of, 9, 26
  venting, 5, 12 and *illus., illus.* 13
  see also baking methods; temperature control of pan

e

eggplant Parmesan, 122
egg rolls, 126
  wrapping method, *illus.* 126
equipment, 9-11
  list, 9-10

f

Fahrenheit/Celsius temperatures, 23, *table* 27
fan for heat circulation, 6
"fines herbes," 42
fish, 110-14
  baked with spinach, 112
  fillets, batter-fried, 113
  sauce, 137
  stock, 34
  see also haddock; salmon; sole; tuna
flour, high-gluten, 24
foil covering of Dutch oven cover, 5, 11 and *illus.*
food:
  substitutions, *table* 21-2
  warming, 19-20
French bread, 142
frostings:
  chocolate mallow, 163
  honey egg, 162

fruit:
  breads (hint), 140
  cake, 156
  and chicken, baked, 92
  crisp, 173
  see also apple; blackberry; blueberry; cherry; date;
    pineapple; raspberry
fudge cake, 158

g

gingerbread, 158
graham cracker crust, 45
gravy, from stock, 33
green bean casserole, 133
ground beef, *see* hamburg

h

haddock:
  baked, 110
  batter-fried, 113
ham:
  baked, 83
  boiled dinner, 72
  and corn chowder, 54
  croquettes, 84
  and rabbit in wine custard, 101
  with scalloped potatoes, 86
  with scalloped squash, 136
hamburg:
  in beef and biscuit topsy-turvy, 75
  in cabbage soup, 52
  in cheeseburger pie, 68
  in chili, 78
  dinner, 73
  Italian meat and potato casserole, 76
  meatballs, 117
  meatloaf, 71
  in rice casserole, 73
  shepherd's pie, 74
  in sloppy Joes, 78
  in spaghetti sauce, 116
  and vegetable soup, 51
hash, corned beef, 76
heat control, *see* temperature control
herb(s):
  bread, 141
  homemade mixes, 42
honey:
  -banana bread, 148
  brownies, 165
  and cooking-time for recipes, 24
  -date cake, 157
  -egg frosting, 162
  -soy chicken, 90
  and tomatoes, scalloped, 138
hors d'oeuvres:
  cream puffs, 46
  fish, 113
horseradish sauce, 38

i

Italian dishes, 115-22

Italian meat and potato casserole, 76
Italian pot roast of beef, 68

l

lemon meringue pie, 169
lentil soup, with sausage, 56
lobster:
  Newburg, 111
  in seafood thermidor pie, 105

m

macaroni:
  and cheese, 120, 121
  with pork chops and tomatoes, 82
  in spaghetti soup, 62
main dishes:
  beef, 64-78
  fish, 110-14
  Italian, 115-22
  meatless, 123-8
  pork, 79-87
  poultry and rabbit, 88-103
  seafood, 104-9
meat:
  -balls, 117
  cooking hints, 23, 26
  leftovers, diced (hint), 67
  loaf, 71
  stuffing for, 41
  thermometer, placement, 23, *illus.* 24, *illus.* 95
  see also specific meats, e.g. beef
meatless meals:
  main dishes, 123-8
  soups, 58-62
metal rack, *see* rack (metal)
metric measurements, *table* 27
minestrone, 55
mixes:
  biscuit, 44
  seasonings, 42
  stuffing, 41
muffins, bran, 149
mushroom(s):
  sauce, 60
  with scalloped clams, 106
  soup, cream of, 60
mustard orange sauce (hot), 38

n

noodle(s):
  with beef, spicy, 69
  with butter and cheese, 123
  in chicken soup, 50
  with pot roast, 68
  -tuna casserole, 113

o

omelet, cheese, 124
onion(s):
  baked stuffed, 135
  and cheese strata, 125

-clam quiche, 109
  rings, fried, 134; in green bean casserole, 133
open-fire cooking, 8 and *illus.*
orange mustard sauce (hot), 38
orange tea rolls, 144
oven, stovetop, *see* Dutch oven
oven thermometer, 10 and *illus.*
  placement for testing Dutch oven, 15 and *illus.*
  placement for testing roaster, *illus.* 18, *illus.* 19

p

pans for stovetop baking, 9
  see also Dutch oven
pan-top thermometer:
  for Dutch oven, *illus.* 15, 16 and *illus.*, 26
  for roaster, *illus.* 19
paper towel method of baking, 22-3 and *illus.*
pasta:
  drying in quantity (hint), 115
  equivalents, *table* 115
  homemade, 115
  sauce for, 117
  see also macaroni; noodles; spaghetti
pastry, 43-6
  pizza crust, 118
pea(s):
  soup, with sausage balls, 53
  sugar snap variety, 61, 88
  with tuna, creamed, 114
pepper steak, 77
piecrust, 44, 45
  graham cracker, 45
  for pizza, 118
  tips on, 43
pies (dessert), 167-70
  apple, 167
  baking temperature for, 7, 25-6
  berry, 168
  blueberry, 168
  coconut custard, 170
  lemon meringue, 169
  pumpkin, 170
pies (main dish):
  cheeseburger, 68
  onion clam quiche, 109
  pizza, 118-19
  rabbit and pork, 98-9
  seafood thermidor, 104-5
pineapple upside-down cake, 160
pizza, 119
  crust, 118
popovers, 145
pork, 79-86
  baked stuffed steak, 79
  and broccoli, stir-fried, 74
  chops, with macaroni and tomatoes, 82
  loaf, jellied, 81
  as pepper steak, 77
  and rabbit pie, 98-9
  roast, 80
  spareribs, sweet and sour, 85
  see also ham; sausage
potato(es):
  Anna style, 131

baked, 132
and meat casserole, Italian, 76
scalloped, with ham, 86
slices, seasoned, 132
pot roast, Italian, 68
poultry, 88-103
  meat thermometer, placement for roasting, *illus.* 95
  seasoning, homemade, 42
  stuffing for, 41
  see also chicken; duckling; turkey
pound cake, 154
preheating Dutch oven, 16, 18, 23
puddings, 171-5
  apple, 171
  banana, 147
  chocolate float, baked, 172
  date, 172
  fruit crisp, 173
  rice, 175
  Thanksgiving, 174
pumpkin pie, 170
Pyrex baking dishes, 10

q

quiche, onion clam, 109

r

rabbit:
  fricasseed, 99
  fried, 102
  and ham in wine custard, 101
  in jellied pork loaf, 81
  and pork pie, 98-9
  with scalloped squash, 136
  sweet and sour, 103
  in wine sauce, 100
  see also recipes for chicken
rack (metal):
  in Dutch oven, 11 and *illus.*, 26 and *illus.*
  placement for roasting beef, *illus.* 65
  in roaster, *illus.* 19, *illus.* 26
  as trivet, 7 and *illus.*, 8
raspberry teacake, 161
recipes:
  adapting, 12, 14, 20, 25
  substituting ingredients, *table* 21-2
refueling stove, 6, 7, 8
ribs, *see* spareribs
rice:
  casserole, 73
  fried, 127
  pudding, 175
  -tuna supper, 114
roaster:
  preparation for baking, 14 and *illus.*; *illus.* 26
  selection of, 9
  temperature testing, 16, *illus.* 18, 19 and *illus.*, *table*
  venting, 14 and *illus.*
rolls:
  beaten batter, 143
  orange tea, 144
roux, 35

s

salmon loaf, 110
sauces, 36-9
  chocolate, 163
  creamed, from soup purées (hint), 36
  fish, 37
  horseradish, 38
  mushroom, 60
  orange mustard (hot), 38
  sweet and sour, 39
  tomato, *see* tomato(es): sauces
  velouté, 36, 37
  white, 36
sausage:
  in baked stuffed onions, 135
  in baked stuffed zucchini, 87
  balls, with split pea soup, 53
  and lentil soup, 56
  with scalloped corn, 85
  in stuffing for meat and poultry, 41
seafood, 104-9
  casserole, 108
  in Chinese egg rolls, 126
  Newburg, 111
  thermidor pie, 104-5
  see also clam(s); crab; fish; lobster; shrimp
seasonings:
  ''fines herbes,'' 42
  poultry, 42
shepherd's pie, 74
shrimp:
  -cauliflower supreme, 107
  Newburg, 111
  in seafood casserole, 108
  and sugar snap peas, stir-fried, 88
sloppy Joes, 78
softwood in stove, 7
sole:
  baked with spinach, 112
  batter-fried, 113
  fillet, Newburg, 111
  in seafood thermidor pie, 105
soups, 48-56
  boiled dinner, 52
  cabbage, 52
  chicken, 50
  corn and ham chowder, 54
  crabmeat bisque, 48
  hamburger vegetable, 51
  lentil, with sausage, 56
  meatless, 58-62; asparagus, cream of, 58; broccoli
    cheese, 58; celery, cream of, 59; mushroom, cream
    of, 60; spaghetti, 62; sugar snap peas, creamed, 61;
    tomato cheese, 61
  minestrone, 55
  puréed for cream sauces (hint), 36
  split pea, 53
  tuna chowder, 49
  see also stocks
spaghetti:
  -chicken bake, 91
  sauce, 116
  soup, 62
spareribs:

beef: in boiled dinner, 72; Italian style, 68
  pork, sweet and sour, 85
spinach, with baked sole, 112
split pea soup with sausage balls, 53
spray-on vegetable coating, 24
squash (butternut), baked with apples, 138
squash (summer), scalloped, 136
stir-fried meals:
  beef and broccoli, 74
  chicken and sugar snap peas, 88
  fried rice, 127
stocks, 32-4
  beef, 32
  chicken, 33
  fish, 34
  when to make, 32
stove:
  fan for heat circulation (hint), 6
  operation, 6-8
  refueling, 6, 7, 8
  surface temperature control, *illus.* 7, 8
stovestack thermometer, 10 and *illus.*
  placement, 15 and *illus.*, *illus.* 19
stovetop baking, *see* baking methods
stovetop thermometer, 10 and *illus.*
  placement, 15 and *illus.*, *illus.* 19
stuffing:
  for meat and poultry, 41
  mix, homemade, 41
substitution of ingredients, *table* 21-2
sugar cookies, 165
sugar snap peas:
  and chicken, stir-fried, 88
  soup, creamed, 61
sweet and sour:
  rabbit, 103
  sauce, 39
  spareribs, 85
Swiss steak, 70

t

temperature:
  Fahrenheit/Celsius, 23, *table* 27
temperature chart:
  for Dutch oven, 15-16, *table* 17, 18 and *table*
  for roaster, 19 and *illus.*, *table*
temperature control of pan, 3, 6, 14-15
  over open fire, 8 and *illus.*
  testing Dutch oven, 15-18 and *tables*
  testing roaster, 16, *illus.* 18, 19 and *illus.*, *table*
  with trivet, *illus.* 7, 8
  see also thermometers; venting
temperature control of stove, 6-8; *see also* thermometers
testing pan and stove temperatures, 15-19 and *tables*
Thanksgiving pudding, 174
thermometers, 10 and *illus.*
  meat, 23, *illus.* 24, *illus.* 95
  placement for testing Dutch oven, 15-16 and *illus.*
  placement for testing roaster, *illus.* 18, *illus.* 19
thermos jug, for warming food, 20
tomato(es):
  -cheese soup, 61
  honeyed, scalloped, 138
  with pork chops and macaroni, 82

sauces: with cheese, 61; for pasta, with meatballs, 117; for pizza, 119; for spaghetti, 116; sweet and sour, 39
and scalloped corn, 137
top-loading stove, refueling of, 8
topping, buttered crumb, 40
tripod, 8 and *illus.*
trivets, *illus.* 7, 8, *illus.* 9
tuna:
　chowder, 49
　creamed, with peas, 114
　-noodle casserole, 113
　rice supper, 114
　in seafood thermidor pie, 105
turkey:
　chow mein, 97
　placement of meat thermometer in, *illus.* 95
　roasted, 94-5
　in wine sauce, 100

v

vegetables, 130-8
　baked, 131
　in beef stew, 67
　in boiled dinner, 72
　in Chinese egg rolls, 126
　in fried rice, 127
　and hamburger soup, 51
　juices from (hint), 133
　marinated, 130
　in minestrone, 55
　puréed (hint), 136
　for roast turkey, 94, 95
　in turkey chow mein, 97
　see also asparagus; beans; broccoli; cabbage;
cauliflower; celery; corn; eggplant; onion(s); pea(s); potato(es); pumpkin; spinach; squash; zucchini
vegetarian:
　main dishes, 123-8
　soups, 58-62
velouté sauce, 36, 37
venting, 5, 12
　adapting to other recipes, 12, 14
　position 1, 12 and *illus.*
　position 2, 12, *illus.* 13
　position 3, 12, *illus.* 13, 14
　roaster, 14 and *illus.*
　see also temperature control of pan: testing
Vermont baked squash and apples, 138

w

warming tray, 20
white bread, 141
white cake, 159
white sauce, 36
whole wheat bread, 141
wire rack, *see* rack (metal)
wonton wrappers, 126
wood stove, *see* stove

y

Yorkshire pudding, 65

z

zucchini:
　baked stuffed, 87
　scalloped, 136

1054